Talitha, Cumi!

Tertia Geldenhuys

Barak Publishers

"For I reckon that the sufferings of this present time are not worthy to be compared with the glory which shall be revealed in us." (Romans 8:18 NKJ)

Talitha, Cumi!

Published by Barak Publishers
Copyright © 2015 by Tertia Geldenhuys

All rights reserved. No part of this book may be produced or transmitted in any form or by any means, electronic or mechanical, including photocopying, recording, or by any information storage and retrieval system, without permission in writing from the author.

Printed by Lulu Press, United States of America
www.lulu.com

ISBN 978-0-9942188-0-3

Contact the author at barakpublishers@gmail.com

TABLE OF CONTENTS

Introduction   7

PART ONE - LEAVING EGYPT, A LAND OF MEAT

Prologue		15
Chapter 1	This is my life!	19

PART TWO – HOW MUCH SUFFERING?

Chapter 2	Lifeline.	33
Chapter 3	Ichabod.	53
Chapter 4	The chosen one.	75
Chapter 5	The land of Moriah.	93

PART THREE – LIVING WATER IN DESERT CIRCLES

Chapter 6	The floodplain of the Jordan.	127
Chapter 7	A sound from Heaven.	155
Chapter 8	The highway of Holiness.	177

PART FOUR – ENTERING THE PROMISED LAND

Chapter 9	My heritage, reward and arrows.	201
Chapter 10	The Sun of Righteousness.	219
Epilogue		231

INTRODUCTION

I knew a woman who once saw a vision of Jesus. After the death of her husband, she cried out to God in her loneliness and begged Him for comfort. He appeared to her one night while she was sitting at her kitchen table. That night changed her life forever. She now tells everyone: "I have seen Jesus! I have seen Jesus!"

I always longed for a better life, a life in abundance. I knew that Jesus was the answer, but I could not see Him. I looked everywhere for Jesus. I tried to find Him in visions; in the fitness of my body and with my intellect by studying many books; I tried to find Him in the arms of love, but He was nowhere to be found.

Then He appeared to me in the blood and sepsis, the stitches and the pain of a little girl He gave to me, my daughter, Resje (pronounced *Reesha*). He touched my eyes and ears, my mouth and heart; He touched my life through her multiple operations. Now I, too, am a changed person and can testify that I have seen Jesus. I saw Him, crucified on a hill with a crown of thorns and bleeding wounds. Now I know for sure that He will come to fetch me one day, the slain Lamb, the Lion of Judah, riding on His white horse with the wind blowing through His hair.

Jesus gave me life through the suffering and agony of my daughter. This is my story of how Jesus took me by the hand and said to me:

"Talitha, cumi…little girl, I say to you, arise."

(Mark 5:41, NKJ)

May our Heavenly Father bless each one who gave me food and water on my journey. Look how strong it made me! My prayer is that everyone who reads this book will find in it some nourishment for the journey of life.

ACKNOWLEDGEMENTS

So many people have journeyed with me. It is impossible to thank everyone personally– please know that you are precious to me and to God who knows who you are.

I would particularly like to express my heartfelt thanks and appreciation to:

My husband, Charl - the anchor of my life.

My son, Emil - God is the Light, you are the light of my life.

Every member of my family - I could not have done this without you. You are the backbone of my life.

My father and mother - no parent could do what you two have done.

Toetie, JP, Magda, Dries, Tina – God has seen your tears and heard your prayers.

My parents-in-law, Igne, Surika, Louis, Lenie – your prayers and encouragement have carried us.

Also to my beloved extended family – your love and acceptance have lifted us.

Every member of my spiritual family - pastors, cell group leaders, brothers and sisters in Christ, everyone who prayed with me and for us - you have given me a reason to carry on. You are the rhythm of my life.

Friends – You have given me space to be me. You are blessings in my life.

Hilary. I could not have done this without you. Thank you for every minute you spent working on my manuscript, encouraging me, crying with me. What an amazing woman of God you are.

Philip and Hanlie. Everything I know, you have taught me. You are forever deep in my heart.

Rob and Hilary. Your love taught me the truth of 1 Cor 13, that love is the greatest of all things.

My prayer partners: Louisa, Linde, Anne, Mona, Janette, Doreen, Aneen, Phillip. I salute you, mighty warriors. The victory belongs to you!

Ngaire Hunt, Justin and Patty Westhuizen. Thank you for much appreciated advice and proofreading.

Every doctor, plastic surgeon, dermatologist, hospital and nursing staff in Resje's life, especially Koos Scholtz (you are the very best!) and Sally Langley.

To the King of kings and Lord of lords - You are my God and my Saviour, my Eagle. Soli Deo Gloria.

I would like to dedicate this book to my daughter Resje, the heartbeat of my life. You changed my whole world. Through Jesus I found Life; through you - life.

PART ONE

LEAVING EGYPT, A LAND OF MEAT.

PROLOGUE

"Then He took the child by the hand, and said to her: 'Talitha, cumi,' which is translated, 'Little girl, I say to you, arise.' Immediately the girl arose and walked, for she was twelve years of age. And they were overcome with great amazement. But He commanded them strictly that no one should know it, and said that something should be given her to eat."

(Mark 5:41-43 (NKJ))

God: Talitha, cumi…

I: How can You say that? How can You say that to *me*?

God: I have always said My grace is sufficient for you.

I: Yes, I know. Now You say to *me* I must arise. I am not the one who needs a touch from You. It is Resje. She is the little girl that needs healing. She is the one that has had seventy-four operations. Your Talitha was a mere 12-year-old girl. Even Resje is older than that. I am too old to arise.

God: You are my Talitha…

I: I do not understand You.

God: I am the One who gives wisdom and understanding and life to those needing it.

I: Then please explain to me why You have not healed my little girl. I have cried out to You for so many years, begging for a miraculous healing. Not for my sake, but for the child You gave to me. I have believed with all my heart that You would heal her. It is more than twenty years later and although You have been with us and carried us all these years, You have still not chosen to heal her. We have forsaken the ways of the world. We have repented from all our sins and iniquities, broken off all curses and chosen to follow You and Your ways. Why are You not stretching Your Hand out towards Resje? One stretch, oh God, has been the plea of my heart all these years. Abba Father, as I am writing this it is still my heart's cry. Not even a touch, a mere thought will suffice, oh, Father God, Lord of our lives!

God: Talitha, cumi!

I: I know You are the Potter and we are the clay. I know I cannot ask why You have made her this way. I beg You to end her suffering. I have no strength to go on. Prophesies and promises have faded. Dreams and hopes lie shattered. Words of encouragement provide temporary relief. My prayers remain unanswered, faith and fantasy blend. During her forty-eighth operation, I was sure that You told me through Your Word that it was the last one. She has just had her seventy fourth. Seventy four operations, God! How can I understand You, Your promises?

God: It is only when you arise, my daughter, that you will receive the strength and wisdom to look through my eyes.

I: If I look through Your eyes, time is of no consequence.

God: What else do you see?

I: I see the beginning. I am too tired to see the end.

God: Then start at the beginning.

I: Who would be interested to read about our suffering? Suffering saturates the world. People struggle with their own loads. I do not comprehend the purpose of suffering. I have no answers.

God: That is what I have been waiting for. Arise, eat, replenish and grow strong. I want you to proclaim My glory. I want you to honour Me, lift up My Name, exalt and love Me.

I: How can I do that if You still have not healed Resje?

God: But I have healed you!

I: I do not feel healed. I feel broken and beaten and I cry all day long. I feel old and tired and without any strength. I mourn not only for my daughter, but also for the death of all my dreams, desires and hope in a better future. Who would want to follow You if Your followers are empty and broken? How can I honour

You, lift up Your name, exalt You or love You if I feel like this?

God: It is when you are empty of yourself, your understanding, securities and words, that I can use you. I had to wait for a very long time for you to reach this point. My power flows strongest when you have given up on yourself and your ideas. You thought you were wise and that you knew all the answers. You thought if you started serving me, you could snap your fingers and I would obey. Your thoughts have resulted in tears and frustration. You have eventually after all these years and operations reached your own deathbed. Now that you are dying to yourself, your hopes and dreams, I can touch you and bring My life forth in you, so that you can glorify Me.

I: I still do not understand.

God: Trust Me! I long to give you the wings of an eagle so that you can soar higher.

> "If you have run with the footmen, and they have wearied you, then how can you contend with horses? And if in the land of peace, in which you trusted, they wearied you, then how will you do in the floodplain of the Jordan?" (Jeremiah 12:5, NKJ)

I: I have nothing to lose, have I?

God: Talitha, cumi!

Chapter One

THIS IS MY LIFE!

From my earliest childhood memories, I can remember God being part of my life. I grew up in a Christian home in South Africa, being the third daughter of four children. My father was a deacon and progressed to elder in a traditional church. In my family, church and Sunday school were priorities. I always believed God existed. I confessed with my lips that Jesus died for my sins, said my prayers, read the Bible every day and attended church even after leaving home.

I studied at a well-known university in the Seventies and did a few post-graduate degrees. I saw myself as privileged and successful and was grateful for the opportunities. I became a University Lecturer, earning a good income. Life was there for me to live to the full. I was busy, carefree, happy and on the go. I chose my friends carefully. They had to be intelligent, of good character, well-developed personalities, idealistic, friendly and helpful; in short, they had to be good people. However, smoking cigarettes, pipe smoking, drinking wine and sleeping with our boyfriends were part of our lifestyles. We all came from a Christian upbringing, but hey, we believed in a merciful God full of forgiveness. You are only young once and our philosophy was to get as much experience from life as possible and then one day to marry decent, good husbands.

We spent hours debating the issues of life. Spiritual subjects were as popular as world events. Our favourite pastime was to spend nights having intellectual discussions about any subject we could think of over a few glasses of wine. We were all working, studying, falling in and out of love, young, happy, carefree, satisfied with life. Because we were law-abiding citizens, caring for one another I regarded us as "good" people. We never seemed to be rude to anyone and never fought. We were neither angry, nor bitter. We were a stimulating group of friends, encouraging and loving one another. I wanted the best out of life. My biggest ambition was to leave a mark on life itself. According to my mom, I came into this world with quite a scream. I did not want to leave quietly.

Sadly, the dreams of my youth did not become the reality I longed for. At the age of 26, I went through a divorce and its subsequent trauma. I had married the love of my life and he had told me that I, too, was the love of his life, but three years later, our love for each other died. The only consolation I had was that we had no children. I became disillusioned with love and life. I became more independent and took the leadership position in our informal discussions about life. I developed a fatalistic life view, decided to sleep even less so as not to miss out on this ever evading life and lived twenty hours a day for years.

At the age of 32, I was a Senior Lecturer at a university. I thought I had the wisdom of King Solomon. I had done some traveling and thought I had seen the world, or the part of the world I had always wanted to see and had done the things I had always wanted to do. I had achieved what I wanted to obtain. I regarded myself as one of the few lucky ones in this life. My dreams and ideals were complete. I found and lost love; I lived life to the full. I was happy to die. I did not have any suicidal thoughts, it was rather a feeling of it was done, finished. I did not exactly leave a mark on life as I wanted to do, but I thought I left a good impression on quite a number of people. To live any longer would have meant a repetition of everything I had done. I did not fancy repetition.

God was always in my life. He was high up in heaven, looking lovingly down on me, His creation. I read my Bible, said my prayers to Father God high up in heaven. When sad, I cried while He comforted me through His Word. I gave Him thirty minutes of my time daily. I went to church, not regularly, but often enough I thought. I gave money to the poor and to the church. I was obedient to the Ten Commandments. I was a divorcee, but I asked God's forgiveness and accepted it through His Son, Jesus Christ. God was most definitely part of my day. I believed I was a Christian and believed that I would go to heaven should I die.

In his famous song, ***My Way***,[1] Frank Sinatra describes exactly how I felt about myself:

> *And now, the end is near,*
> *And so I face the final curtain,*
> *My friend, I'll say it clear;*
> *I'll state my case, of which I'm certain.*
>
> *I've lived a life that's full –*
> *I've traveled each and every highway,*
> *And more, much more than this,*
> *I did it my way.*
>
> *Regrets? I've had a few,*
> *But then again, too few to mention.*

---

[1] Lyrics of "My Way" by Frank Sinatra, www.lyricsfreak.com

I did what I had to do
And saw it through without exemption.

I planned each charted course;
Each careful step along the byway,
But more, much more than this,
I did it my way.

Yes, there were times, I'm sure you knew,
When I bit off more than I could chew,
But through it all, when there was doubt,
I ate it up and spat it out.
I faced it all and I stood tall
And did it my way.

I've loved, I've laughed and cried,
I've had my fill – my share of losing,
And now, as tears subside,
I find it all so amusing.

To think I did all that
And may I say - not in a shy way,
No. Oh no, not me.
I did it my way.

For what is a man, what has he got?
If not himself, then he has naught.
To say the things he truly feels;
And not the words of one who kneels,

The record shows I took the blows -
And did it my way.

Yes, it was my way.

One of my few regrets was that I did not really succeed in keeping love. I kept falling in and out of love. Broken relationships shattered me. After another unsuccessful relationship, my heart was in pieces. I was adamant never to fall in love again.

In desperation, my prayers to God became more fervent. I earnestly asked Him to keep me away from disastrous relationships. I made a half-hearted commitment to read more of the Bible, to pray longer and harder. I know now that the commitment was empty words but one request I remember clearly. I remember saying to God that my attempt to live life to the full felt meaningless. I asked Him to change me and to lead me to the meaningful destiny and purpose that had constantly evaded me.

A second marriage at the age of 32 was completely unplanned. I had thought that my life's agenda was finished. I thought it foolish to fall in love and to get married again, yet I still went ahead. Then it happened. I fell pregnant - too soon. By the time we had been married five months, I was already two months pregnant. Because I was spiritually dead, my flesh rebelled against this new life growing inside me. I hated everything with a passion: I hated the pregnancy, gaining weight, feeling sick and maternity clothes. I blamed my husband, Charl, for being the cause of this dreaded situation. Everything about this pregnancy was wrong. The timing was wrong. The sex was wrong. Although the gynaecologist did not want to disclose the sex of the baby, Charl and I had both seen that it was a boy during the scans. I did not like boys. If ever I wanted a baby I would have wanted a girl. Falling pregnant was a full-scale disaster!

My independent existence had not prepared me to take care of a dependent, demanding human being who needed to be taught everything. My forte was teaching students the art of literature, not teaching babies how to stop crying and when to poo.

I controlled the sceptre over my life. I held it in my hand. Now my more experienced friends tried to prepare me for how this sceptre would need to diminish. I had dark depressing thoughts about the consequences of this new lifestyle.

I cancelled the PhD research I was doing on the stage drama for another major theatrical production was going on in my head and body! The gynaecologist could not understand why. His exact words were: "Pregnancy does not clog up your brain!" I thought what a daft gynaecologist. What does he know! I sat in front of my desk thinking of nothing else than this fetus growing bigger and bigger. I became obsessed with how my life was going to change and how I was going to loose my identity, personality, independence, job, my figure – myself!

I was so upset about the pregnancy that our family doctor suggested an abortion for my mental well-being. Mercifully, the Author of Life immediately erased that idea from my mind.

I blamed God for the pregnancy. It was first of all Charl's fault, and then God's. He could have prevented it. Charl, being a farmer, knew how precious life was. He was thrilled with my pregnancy, but he dared not show me how he felt. Charl's suppressed joy and excitement and the GP's concern about my mental state of mind, caused me to hide my true feelings. I bought and played all the classical music tapes that a pregnant mother should play to her baby, I started stroking my ever expanding stomach and spoke to the baby. I smiled to all the onlookers and stopped complaining. My head and my heart were boiling though, deep inside, where nobody could see.

The baby was actively living out my feelings. It kicked constantly. I thought the baby was complaining about this pregnancy too. It wanted out. I read about the psychological effects of rejection on the fetus. Abortion was not an option. I was so healthy that a miscarriage was unthinkable. God was not going to end this pregnancy. There was only one thing for me to do. I had to go through with it.

My view of life changed, as well as my moods and my body. My life changed. As my body became heavier, my heart became darker. Something was happening to me over which I had no control. That infuriated me. Maybe, I thought, this would indeed be the end of my life. Not the way I wanted it to end. I wanted it to end with a proper, romantic funeral with lots of reading, singing and dancing. In my mind, I could hear the eulogies of what I had achieved in my life from all the many people I had touched and enriched.

A dark premonition evolved that this would mean the end of everything I had believed in. I had come across many people who walk and talk, but their eyes are dead because of living in a hell. I thought this was going to happen to me. I would still be alive, take in oxygen, talk and eat, but my eyes and heart would be dead. Thinking of this baby and how it was going to affect my life was already hell for me. I knew deep down in my heart that I had reached the end of a dispensation. From now on, there would be a new order and I would no longer rule there. People tried to console me with the usual know-it-all-comments: "You are only scared of the unknown"; "things will look better as soon as the baby is born"; "cheer up, your life is not going to end"; "you are going to love this baby", ad nauseam.

I had reached the back door of the room containing all the dreams and desires for my life. At first, I was in control of my world. This was my existence, my safe haven. Then, suddenly, my world was crushed as one would crush an insect. Was that God's modus operandi? Did He take the sceptre out of my hand and wave it off to a distant dispensation. I had no choice in this matter. As a mere traveler on the road of life, the route was diverted without any warning. Tough luck mate, from now on you travel on that road over there. The back door of my world opened up and I was pushed out. I had a nine-month free fall, down to a new order.

I had not wanted to marry a second time or to fall pregnant. Because I did, I had to blame someone, avoiding the responsibilities for my own actions. It was easier for me to blame God. At 32, I did not regard new life as a blessing from God. In fact, it was quite the opposite. I saw my pregnancy as a curse. I wanted a change in my life, but I wanted it on my terms. I thought God was jealous of my carefree existence, wanting to change me via this pregnancy by driving a nail through me, crushing me, punishing me. This was unfair.

Despite the anger and bitterness within, gradually guilt grew.

Maybe I did not give You the attention and time You expected. Maybe You had other ideas for my life, and I went ahead and did it my way. Maybe I took life's glory entirely for myself and gave You nothing. In any case, what did You think I meant when I asked You to change me in order to reach fulfillment?

Throughout the nine months of pregnancy, awareness grew that something in me had to die for this baby to live. Instinctively I realized I had to surrender my dreams and ambitions. My rebelliousness argued that although not everything in my life was perfect, it certainly was not all that wrong. People, more sinful than I, were living happily in their old lifestyles. I wanted God to remain on His heavenly throne, looking after me, not to come down and interfere with my life.

The gynaecologist decided on an induction on 31 August 1988, two days after our first wedding anniversary. My whole body was swollen, for my due date had come and gone without any sign that the baby had any intention of coming out. I lay there on the hospital bed, thinking that my heart had died. My spirit was dead. Somewhere I had read that a stained spirit is a dead spirit. I wondered what would a stained spirit look like. I thought of my heart, the centre of my soul and thought of the stains on it. In my mind's eye, I could see the stains. They looked like blemishes, like dark spots. My heart was full of black marks. The heart is the place where you find love and life. I thought of how many times I thought I had found love, only to lose it again. I did not have any love for this baby. There was no real life left in me. My heart became one huge black mark, flowing over its edges.

The backbone of my spirit, the source of encouraging and uplifting others, including my spiritual arms and legs were covered with black, deep rooted blemishes obstructing and interfering in my relationship with God. Little black spots influenced the visual and auditory senses of my spirit. My very soul was contaminated to the extent where the intimate sharing with my soul mate was affected.

I could hide the black marks in the depths of my heart and soul. In my relationship with Christians, I only exposed a fraction of the light inside me. My black marks were well camouflaged by the darkness of the world. The blemishes were like a curse. My soul was in agony. There on the hospital bed while the gynaecologist was initiating the induction, I contemplated the state of my inner self. What I saw disturbed me intensely. I cried out to the Light. Darkness, however beckoned me to escape, to run away and hide from the light.

As I progressively refrained from openly rejecting the baby and not allowing myself to voice my anger, disappointment and fear, so an irritation inside my heart escalated. It was as if all the blemishes were inflamed, developing into an evil infection, a deep internal secret. God was the only other being who knew of my hidden turmoil. I thought He did not care and therefore blamed Him for not providing an antidote. With the baby, the darkness grew. With the darkness, a rebellious irritation developed.

The birthing process was about to start when I realized I had never bowed down to honour, serve or love God. I brought Him no glory, as I did not know Him. I knew of Him as the Creator of the heavens and the earth. I knew of Him as the Father who took His Son's blood as payment for all our sins. It felt as though God was about to take my joy of life as payment for this new baby.

I had no desire to start serving Him or loving Him there on that hospital bed. I was angry with Him. I was disillusioned. I wanted to do it all my way, but God had interfered.

What made me persevere was the knowledge that eventually I had to give birth to a life. From the first flutter of life, there was continuous kicking and movement. With each consultation the doctor commented about this extremely active baby. Deep inside I knew what the reason was - life can only clash with death if contained in the same body. My spiritual lifelessness contrasted with this abundant life. A new physical and spiritual life was waiting to see the light. I felt that the baby was a separate entity, complete with his own body and spirit. I remembered reading how John the Baptist, being filled with the Holy Spirit, leapt in his mother's womb when he heard Mary's voice. The time was ripe for separation.

They broke my waters. They inserted a huge, thick needle and stabbed me. As the waters gushed out of me, I smelled something bitter. I knew the waters were filled with my dreams, hopes and desires.

I had a vague picture at the back of my mind of a soldier piercing Jesus' side and waters gushing out of Him. Unlike Frank Sinatra, Jesus, too, had to give up His way. Could it be that He understood what was going on inside me? And if He did, did He care?

I shut my eyes. I had no choice. My way was blocking the baby's path. And the baby was stronger than me. I was forced to give up… to make way.

PART TWO

HOW MUCH SUFFERING?

Chapter Two

LIFELINE

> "Then the king was deeply moved, and went up to the chamber over the gate, and wept. And as he went, he said thus: 'O my son Absalom – my son, my son Absalom – if only I had died in your place! O Absalom my son, my son!'"(2 Samuel 18:33, NKJ)

Only a loving, forgiving parent can understand this cry from King David. In our broken world it is very difficult to love someone until death do us part. It is even more difficult to lay down your life for a certain person. Maybe there are people, who will willingly lay down their lives for someone who has a kind heart or someone who is exceptionally good, loyal and faithful. I do not think anyone would want to die for someone as cunning and cruel as Absalom – except maybe his father, or his mother.

In this passage in the Bible, David's son, Absalom, became obsessed with power. He was not happy to be only a prince. He wanted to become king. He wanted to have the same status as his father, but his father was still young, strong and popular, loved by his people.

Absalom was rebellious. He desired power and esteem. He wanted to do everything in his power to have the crown on his own head. He listened to the wrong advice and made evil plans. At first, he slept with his father's concubines to cause animosity between him and his father, and then he planned to murder his father in cold blood.

Absalom was truly a dangerous character, an arch-scoundrel and a murderer.

His death suited him fine. He fled on a mule, not a strong, royal horse. The mule ran under the thick boughs of a large oak tree and in the process Absalom's hair got tangled in the branches, leaving him hanging between heaven and earth. It is ironical that his natural crown, his long beautiful hair, caused his death. He must have suffered excruciating pain, defeat and humility while hanging there. Joab found him alive and pierced Absalom's heart with three spears, bringing a humiliating end to his life – a deserving dishonourable death. In Galatians 3:13 and Deuteronomy 21:23 we read that everyone who hangs from a tree is cursed by God. Absalom died hanging on a tree, alone and cursed by God. He had to pay for his rebelliousness, his strife for power and his murderous heart. Years later, Jesus was crucified on a tree. He had to pay for our rebelliousness and strife, for our murderous hearts, sin and shame, cursed by God.

However, Absalom had a father, David, the mighty King of Israel. David forgave his son. He mourned his death, wishing he could die in Absalom's place. With David's cry of forgiveness, we can understand why he became a man after God's own heart. David had the godly ability to forgive his own rebellious son. As parents, we do the same. We look at our rebellious children, many of them drug addicts, alcoholics, and we love them, we forgive them, we wish that we could carry some of their load to make it easier for them. We look at our sick and suffering children and we wish that we could take the hurt away from them. As parents, we want the best for our children.

When I went to reserve my hospital bed months before the baby was born, the staff showed me the maternity ward and told me that the custom of the hospital in Durban, South Africa, was to put the naked, unwashed baby onto the mother's breast immediately after cutting the umbilical cord.

Because this unwanted pregnancy was gnawing at my conscience, I somehow believed that this would be a miraculous moment. My knowledge of psychology endorsed the importance of the bonding process in the mother-child relationship. Despite the fact that I did not bond with the baby in my womb, I always desired to have children of my own, wanting a special bond similar to that which I had with my mother. I hoped that the wet, naked body of the baby against my breast would be the magic wand that would bring on the emotional bonding that is so critically important in the field of psychology.

When God walked in the Garden of Eden, just after the Serpent had successfully infiltrated the future of mankind, God turned to Eve and said:

> "I will greatly multiply your sorrow and your conception: In pain you shall bring forth children; your desire shall be for your husband, and he shall rule over you." (Genesis: 3:16, NKJ)

When the first contractions started, I thought I was not going to make it. No doctor, book, or video prepares you for childbirth. The only thing that kept me going was the one phrase that I repeated a million times: "Never again, never again, never again…" I could not believe that it was possible to endure so much pain. How much suffering can a human being endure? How could this God who punished Eve so severely for one disobedient deed be the same God who sent His Son to earth because of His love for us? Where was His love when Eve sinned? Was that not the time when she needed love and acceptance? How many more women in the generations to come will have to pay the price for Eve's sin?

I was more disobedient and distant in my relationship with Him than Eve. I have never walked with Him in the Garden of Eden like Eve. How could I ever be part of God's love and grace? If I understand Genesis 3 correctly, it means that it is God's will for me to have this excruciating pain. Can a God of love punish a woman so much? Can a God of love keep punishing women through all these centuries? Is the softness of a woman, the warmth of her love not enough reason for God to revoke this curse? Why does He not end this senseless pain and suffering?

God says that children and life are blessings from Him. In the Fifth Commandment, God promises the prolonging of life for those who honour their fathers and mothers. Yet, there are so many people on this earth with physical and emotional scars because of a traumatic birth. There are people who feel unwanted when they enter this world; who think they are born the wrong sex; who stay strangers for the rest of their lives, not conforming to society. They are the key subjects of psychologists, therapists and counsellors. The umbilical cord binding you to your origin is cut off in one second. Moreover, when you leave the world one day, the umbilical cord that binds you with this world is also severed in a moment. It is a mess when you are born and it is a mess when you die.

I had to die to my own pain to bring forth life. To deliver the baby an episiotomy, tearing and forceps were necessary. I could not understand why it was such a struggle for the baby to leave his unwelcome, dark womb. What was it that held the baby captive in that darkness? Was it the feeling of not wanting to abandon his place of security, or the fear of the unknown and the light?

I had to burst open like an overripe pomegranate to tear loose the bruised seed.

With only its head out, the baby started crying. It was not the usual cry to celebrate life but piercing screams, hailing the beginning of a nightmare. It was much later that I understood the reluctance of the baby to be born. The baby was protesting against the nine months of hell it had experienced in the womb and screaming for the hell that lay ahead.

As the doctor pulled out the rest of the body, Charl's voice came to me: "Ters, dit is 'n dogtertjie!" (Ters [Tertia], it is a little girl).

I do not know whether it was the surprised joy in Charl's voice, feeling joyful for my sake, or whether it was the fact that this baby was indeed a little girl, or whether it was a combination of both, but a tremendous feeling of forgiveness flowed through me. I immediately forgave Charl for causing the pregnancy. I thought somewhere during my pregnancy God must have realized a little girl would make me happy, so I immediately forgave God for allowing this pregnancy.

I desperately wanted to feel her naked, unwashed body against my skin. I wanted her to know that all my thoughts and words were completely wrong, to hold her and ask for forgiveness. The unwashed blood, the proof of life was part of me. I desperately wanted to bond with her.

A nurse immediately wrapped her in a sheet and put her against my breast. I thought this nurse must be new and that she was not familiar with the hospital's regulations, but I was too exhausted to voice my need. I wanted to take the sheet off and hug the naked baby, but I had no strength. I accepted the little girl in the sheet and bonded with her immediately. My arms around this tiny bundle asked for forgiveness. I felt how all the rejection, anger and bitterness left my heart.

Then she did a strange thing. With all the strength that she had, she pressed up against my breast so that her head and neck straightened up. The gynaecologist called out: "Look at that!" Everyone in the theatre turned and looked at her. It became dead still. You could hear a pin drop. With every bit of effort she had in her body, she lifted her head, and with focused eyes looked me straight in the eye. She had the most beautiful big black eyes with three black beauty spots right next to her right eye on her cheekbone. I looked back and I saw that she had something inside her that I did not have. She was alive. Her eyes were full of forgiveness and love. It was the face of God looking upon me, a sinner full of blemishes. She had a huge vulnerable frown on her face.

Maybe she knew then what agony was awaiting her.

She captivated my eyes. It felt as if she had something within her that was older, wiser and superior to me. The fullness of her eyes absorbed the emptiness of my life. In the distance, I thought I heard a rooster crow and I knew it was the same eyes that looked upon Peter. I felt the tears rolling down my cheeks and I knew I had denied her for nine months. I searched for hurt in her eyes, but all I could see were two huge windows of love and forgiveness.

Much later, I realized that this was the moment when the life and fullness of the Spirit of God touched my emptiness.

In the hushed atmosphere, the hospital staff took her away. My heart started beating faster. Something was wrong. They did not only take my child away; they also took the secret of Life away with them. It was within her, this secret of Life and I knew that I had come close to it. I was petrified that she was going to die. Then, I thought, maybe I was the one who would die. I did not understand what was going on, but I desperately wanted to find out what my baby's secret was.

My maternal instincts erupted. I would fight for her with my naked hands. I would do everything to keep her alive. The mother-child bonding existed because of her eyes, not her naked body. In her eyes was forgiveness for all the wrong things I knowingly and unknowingly did. I would die for her.

People who have had a death or near death experience say that your whole life rolls past you in a flashback. I had two hours of reliving my past, 120 minutes of hell. Everything I saw was empty, without meaning and sinful. I knew that I knew the Way, but that I did not walk it. Because I brought forth life despite my own brokenness and emptiness, I hoped that God would be forgiving and gracious towards me.

Two hours later, a nurse came to the hospital room that I shared with three other mothers. Charl was at my side all the time, not saying much. The nurse said that a paediatrician had requested a private room for me. I was laying flat on my back as she wheeled me to the private room, knowing clearly that I had reached the end of my strength. I had come to a standstill. I knew that no money or wisdom, no confidence or power, could prevent what was waiting for us in that private room. For 33 years I had stood on my own two feet, now I was on my back. I was overcome by something much bigger than I could handle.

It was a long way to the private room, long enough for me to die to myself. I simply said: "Here, God, here is my life. I give you my life. I give you the pathetic bundle that I am. This is all I can give you. I cannot give you any special presents or achievements. I did not use the talents that You gave me. I did not obey You. I am not pure and without sin. I do not know You, Jesus, or the Holy Spirit. I did not meditate on Your Word day and night. You were the Potter in my life but I cannot give You back a work of art. All I can give You is dry clay. I know that what I am about to find out is bigger than what I can handle. Please take over in my life. Take over, God. Take over."

I remembered that Jesus was also 33 years old when He died on the cross at Calvary. Suddenly, it was as clear as daylight to me. Like Jesus, I had to die to everything I thought was life. My idea of life was studying books, gaining more knowledge, exercising my body, traveling, socializing, pursuing love, living for the moment. I had to die to all of this and then descend to hell. I wondered what my hell would be. A paediatrician, a gynaecologist, hospital staff and a little girl were waiting for me in the private room. Will she be my hell? Will this new life be our hell? The good news is that I will be raised after three days as a new person. I wondered how long Jesus' three days in hell would take me. Would it take me longer than three days?

I did not know then that it would take me more than 20 years.

Charl was walking behind me. I could not hear or see him. The nurse did not say a word. I felt alone. I stretched my hand out to touch the hand of Jesus, because I remembered He, too, was alone in Gethsemane. His beloved disciples did not pray with Him. I heard Jesus faintly praying with me: *Father God, take this cup away from me.* I could not carry on, but I thought I heard Jesus say: "Not her will, but Yours be done."

In the anguish of that still dark passage, I thought of the Shunammite woman. She was rich and influential. Every time the prophet, Elisha, visited the town, she hosted him. She had everything in life she wanted, except a child. She never told anyone about this desire and buried it in her heart after experiencing month after month the emptiness and shame of her barrenness. She must have reached a point where she gave up on her dreams and desires or suppressed it to her subconscious mind. To bless her for her hospitality, God, through the prophet Elisha, stretched out His finger and touched her heart to bring that desire and dream to life. A year later, the Shunammite woman gave birth to a son only to see him die a few years later.

I wondered if that was happening to me. Like the Shunammite woman, I too desired life that I buried deep in my heart. When that life burst out of me in the form of my daughter, I tasted it for a few minutes, before she was taken away from me.

However, the Shunammite woman had a fighting spirit. She did not mourn the death of her son. She did not tell anyone that he had died. The umbilical cord between the two of them became too thick for death to cut. Through that umbilical cord, life came to her. Life came into their house and into her heart. She would not give up so easily on that life. She would fight for it with every bit of her being. She went to look for the prophet, the prophet Elisha, the prophet of God.

Elisha thought it was good enough to send his servant, Gehazi, to go to the dead boy and lay his staff on the face of the child. Nevertheless, with the same desperation of the blind Samson who brought down the pillars of the temple, the Shunammite woman persuaded Elisha to come himself.

It was not easy for Elisha to bring the boy back to life. He had to stretch himself twice over the dead boy with his mouth over the boy's mouth, his eyes over the boy's eyes, his hands over the boy's hand. At first, the flesh of the boy became warm, after the second attempt, life flowed back into the boy.

(2 Kings 4)

I realized that I quickly had to find the same strength that this Shunammite woman had. I did not know a prophet of God to fetch. Although it was dead in my own heart, I had seen life in the eyes of my daughter. I could strongly identify with the desire of the Shunammite woman. I remembered another man. He was more than a prophet of God. He was the Son of God. His name was Jesus. I took my hands from under the hospital sheets and opened them. I felt the presence of Jesus folding His Hands over mine and my hands started warming up. The next moment my heart started beating rapidly. It sounded like loud hammer blows, reverberating in my ears. It was as if the whole hospital echoed the throbs. Then it stopped.

The paediatrician and senior medical staff entered the room. Apologetically he informed us that our daughter was born with a skin condition, called giant pigmented naevi - in layman's language giant birthmarks or moles that were skin tumours. An abnormal development in the pigmentation cells during the sixth week of pregnancy was the cause of the condition. Before I could utter a sigh of relief, his next words stabbed my heart. He bore knowledge of this rare condition, but was astounded by its extent in our baby. The naevi were pitch black, extending up to 2.5 cm deep. One gigantic naevus covered her entire back, stretching from the hairline of her neck to her buttocks, wrapping over both sides to the upper front section of her chest. Big naevi, the size of the palm of my hand, were on her legs, knees, buttocks and groin. Multiple smaller naevi were scattered on her head, inside her ears, nose, underneath her feet, on her face, hands, arms, legs, stomach, chest, on her lips, inside her mouth, in the white of her eyes, literally everywhere. She was covered from head to foot, front and back, with dangerous black skin tumours of various dimensions.

I was like a wounded tigress. My baby was not in the room and I wanted to have her. I wanted to hold her and put her to my breast.

A nurse later told me that it was considered best not to have the baby in the room for fear of my reaction.

The truth of the matter was that I wanted to shout for joy at that moment, because I was so relieved that it was only a skin condition. I expected a graver judgment. She was alive and that meant more to me than anything else. In the maternity theatre, I made contact with the Life within her and it drew me like a magnet. She held the keys of the chains around my heart in her dark eyes. She had the answer within her. I knew that the Life in her had the ability to free me, to lead me out of Egypt. I had reached a cross road in my life and I knew instinctively she would be the one to bring me to the Way, the Truth and the Life.

A nurse brought her in and handed her to me. I took my baby girl from her hand, pressing her body against mine, burying my face in hers and cuddling her in my arms before putting her to my breast. There was no need to look at the skin condition straight away. She was more than her skin. This precious moment was more important than exploring a medical condition.

I looked down expectantly on her helpless little mouth searching for nourishment. Like Moses, she was going to lead me into the Promised Land to Jesus, yet she was so small and vulnerable. She had to grow up first and grow strong before she would be able to beat water out of the Rock for me.

I looked underneath her clothes while she was feeding. My first reaction was that it was not as bad as the doctor said. Only the next morning did I take all her clothes off and stare at the naevi. The reality of the condition slowly dawned upon me. It was much worse than what I first saw.

The prognosis enhanced the shock. The naevi had to be removed as quickly as possible. The condition greatly increased the risk of developing into malignant melanoma. If melanoma developed, the deadly cancer could reach the blood stream with fatal consequences.

It turned out to be a race against time. Precious time. Time meant life for her. The dawn of every morning brought her less time to live.

We went searching for help. From God to dermatologists to plastic surgeons; from soap to miracle creams; from one small bit of advice to another little bit of hope; from one reproach to another sense of guilt. I blamed everyone I could think of. I blamed myself and we felt guilty, punished by God. We were angry that God did not punish us for our sins. Why did He punish an innocent little baby? I was shocked to realize that the great Artist took the inner me, my black heart with all its blemishes, and duplicated it on the exterior of my baby for the world to witness.

I read about Miriam. God chose her to take care of her baby brother, Moses, drifting in a basket on the Nile. Years later, when Moses led the Israelites out of Egypt, the prophetess, Miriam, with tambourine and dance, headed the exodus after the Red Sea crossing. Later when Miriam and her brother, Aaron, spoke out against Moses for marrying the Ethiopian woman, God, in His fury, struck Miriam with leprosy. He did not strike Aaron. For reasons known only to God, He chose Miriam and lay upon her flesh His fury and anger. I saw Resje's skin as the outward manifestation of God's anger. I identified very strongly with Aaron's cry when he saw Miriam become leprous in an instant. He cried out to his brother Moses:

> "Oh, my lord! Please do not lay this sin on us, in which we have done foolishly and in which we have sinned. Please do not let her be as one dead, whose flesh is half consumed when he comes out of his mother's womb!" (Numbers 12:11-12, NKJ)

Just like Miriam, Resje's flesh was indeed half consumed when she came out of my womb.

It was a miracle to maintain sanity through all of this. Resje was like an untamed, caged-in, wild animal. The tumours burned and itched constantly. Her agonizing screams never stopped. She could only sleep for two hours at a time. The pattern did not break after the usual six weeks or three months or even a year. It continued for seven and a half long years. That is ninety months. That is two thousand, seven hundred and thirty days and just as many nights. That might have been the reason why she had been so abnormally active during pregnancy. The skin irritation had tormented her even before she was born. After two hours of sleep, the burning and irritation would wake her up. To watch how she tried to relieve the pain asked something of me I did not have. She searched for relief with her eyes, her hands and her voice. She scratched herself until she bled. She sat up straight in her cot with a white cloth nappy in her mouth and like a wild bear continuously rubbed her back against the wooden rungs of the cot. Whenever she was put down, she would immediately lie down on her back and start wriggling her back on the floor, the carpet or grass. Her efforts to relieve the pain were inhumane.

There was no medication, no ointment or lotion that doctors could prescribe to help her. I gently put my hand on her back and on her little neck and stroked her for hour upon hour in an attempt to sooth her, but I could not take the burning or the itching away.

Nearly everyone we met saw this as a curse from God. So did I. I went to God's Word and I read:

> "But it shall come to pass, if you do not obey the voice of the Lord your God, to observe carefully all His commandments and His statutes which I command you today, that all these curses will come upon you and overtake you:
>
> Cursed shall you be in the city, and cursed shall you be in the country.
>
> Cursed shall be your basket and your kneading bowl.
>
> Cursed shall be the fruit of your body and the produce of your land, the increase of your cattle and the offspring of your flocks.
>
> Cursed shall you be when you come in, and cursed shall you be when you go out.
>
> The Lord will send on you cursing, confusion, and rebuke in all that you set your hand to do, until you are destroyed and until you perish quickly, because of the wickedness of your doings in which you have forsaken Me.
>
> The Lord will make the plague cling to you until He has consumed you from the land which you are going to possess.
>
> The Lord will strike you with consumption, with fever, with inflammation, with severe burning fever, with the sword, with scorching, and with mildew; they shall pursue you until you perish."
>
> (Deuteronomy 28:15-22, NKJ)

> "The Lord will strike you with the boils of Egypt, with tumors, with the scab, and with the itch, from which you cannot be healed.

The Lord will strike you with madness and blindness and confusion of heart. And you shall grope at noonday, as a blind man gropes in darkness; you shall not prosper in your ways; you shall be only oppressed and plundered continually, and no one shall save you."

(Deuteronomy 28:27-29, NKJ)

"So you shall be driven mad because of the sight which your eyes see.

The Lord will strike you in the knees and on the legs with severe boils which cannot be healed, and from the sole of your foot to the top of your head."

(Deuteronomy 28:34-35, NKJ)

"Moreover all these curses shall come upon you and pursue and overtake you, until you are destroyed, because you did not obey the voice of the Lord your God, to keep His commandments and His statutes which He commanded you. And they shall be upon you for a sign and a wonder, and on your descendants forever.

Because you did not serve the Lord your God with joy and gladness of heart, for the abundance of everything, therefore you shall serve your enemies, whom the Lord will send against you, in hunger, in thirst, in nakedness, and in need of everything; and He will put a yoke of iron on your neck until He has destroyed you."

(Deuteronomy 28:45-48, NKJ)

"If you do not carefully observe all the words of this law that are written in this book, that you may fear this glorious and awesome name, THE LORD YOUR GOD, then the Lord will bring upon you and your descendants extraordinary plagues – great and prolonged plagues – and serious and prolonged sicknesses. Moreover He will bring back on you all the diseases of Egypt, of which you were afraid, and they shall cling to you.

Also every sickness and every plague, which is not written in this Book of the Law, will the Lord bring upon you until you are destroyed."

(Deuteronomy 28:58-61, NKJ)

"And it shall be, that just as the Lord rejoiced over you to do you good and multiply you, so the Lord will rejoice over you to destroy you and bring you to nothing; and you shall be plucked from off the land which you go to possess." (Deuteronomy 28:63, NKJ)

"Your life shall hang in doubt before you; you shall fear day and night, and have no assurance of life. In the morning you shall say, 'Oh, that it were evening!' And at evening you shall say, 'Oh, that it were morning!' because of the fear which terrifies your heart, and because of the sight which your eyes see."

(Deuteronomy 28:66-67, NKJ)

Yes, we were cursed. We were guilty.

We had sinned and God had cursed us. By cursing our daughter, He cursed us. In the mornings we were exhausted from lack of sleep and from living with a baby who was constantly in agony, screaming out her pain, wishing that it could be night so that we might have two hours of sleep; in the evenings we were exhausted from seeing her pain and not sleeping enough, wishing it was morning. We knew we were cursed. We saw it, we lived under it, and our baby lived in it. I felt guiltier than Charl, and Charl felt guiltier than I did. I wondered what we had done to provoke God to such anger.

Somewhere one of us, or one of our parents, or grandparents, or great grandparents, or great-great grandparents must have done something very sinful to provoke God this much. Does God not clearly state in the Ten Commandments:

> "... For I, the Lord your God, am a jealous God, visiting the iniquity of the fathers upon the children to the third and fourth generations of those who hate Me." (Exodus 20:5, NKJ)

I could not fight the God who had the power to curse us. He was too big for me. He was Almighty and powerful. We were guilty as charged. I learned to survive; I learned to stay sane and I learned to hide many thoughts and feelings. We went to see a Christian therapist. We turned to our family and friends with our pain. We went to our church pastors for prayer. They were all amazing and they were there for us. I would never have been able to write this book without their support, help and prayers, yet they could not undone the hurt. In order to conform to this world with its unwritten rules and regulations on behavior I learned to hide many things. If ever I had dared to scream my pain and anger out to the whole world, as I had wanted to do, I would have been institutionalized. If ever I had dared to tell people I could not carry on seeing my baby living in torment and agony, they would have taken her away from me. I had to suppress my emotions, play them down, pretending that I could handle it all. The many people whom I met, or sometimes just passed by, who were victims of suffering themselves, or were taking care of a sufferer helped me to cope. I instantly recognized in their eyes that they felt exactly as I did. The show must go on. Life does not come to a standstill when somebody dies, or when someone is born blind, or when someone is paralyzed in a swimming pool accident. Life, like God, is too big to fight.

What are we doing to ourselves? It is like fighting a war. We send young soldiers in to a war zone, expecting them to gaze upon fear and death and survive. Then they spend the rest of their lives trying to cope with the anguish they saw. When my father died, my mother was so heavily sedated she fell asleep during the funeral service. We prescribe something for shock, something for depression, calming them: 'Do not cry', when their whole world collapses underneath them. Then years later we spend hours and money on therapy to tell our therapists all our suppressed thoughts and emotions.

When will we start looking upon the One Face of suffering and find the answers there?

I wondered what Absalom was thinking, hanging in that large oak tree, knowing it was impossible for him to cut loose his hair. Did he experience guilt? Did he know that God was mad at him and cursing him for his sin? Was he sorry for what his intentions were? I felt like I think Absalom might have felt. I lived a carefree life like Absalom, full of rebelliousness and wanting to do my own thing. I deserved the pain of God's curse. I was the sinner who wanted to live my life my way. There was no throne in my heart for God. I sat on the throne. Exactly like Absalom, I was not happy to be only a princess – I wanted to be queen. I was the murderer, the rebellious one. My heart was black. A righteous and just God cursed Absalom.

However, unlike Absalom, I was not the one hanging from the oak tree. My daughter was hanging there. The curse of God should have been on my body for everyone to see. How could the wrath of God come onto a helpless baby? She was not guilty. She was innocent. There was nothing I could do to help her. I could not take her marks onto me. I could not donate my skin to her, the doctors advised against it. The risk of rejecting donor skin was unacceptably high. I could not take her irritation and burning on me. I could not help or make it easier for her. I could not take her torment away. Like a newborn lamb, she was caught up in the branches of the large oak tree. There was no Joab to thrust her with his spears.

Death was not an option. She was to hang there on the tree for the whole world to see.

I could only observe. I saw how she went through hell. I looked and had to hide my pain from the rest of the world. I looked and had to stay sane. I looked and had to smile and laugh and go on with my life. I looked and did not allow myself to think of euthanasia. I looked and looked. I saw the most beautiful little girl with the most beautiful eyes, her lovely hair, her beautiful white skin, the perfect body that no-one could see because it was hidden by gigantic life-threatening, burning, itching, black, skin tumours. All I wanted to do was to shout so that the mountains would move:

O, my daughter Resje - my daughter, my daughter Resje – if only I could take your place and take the tumours and the pain on my body! O Resje my daughter, my daughter!

Chapter Three

ICHABOD

Resje needed urgent treatment. Three weeks after she was born, we made appointments with all the dermatologists and plastic surgeons in the Durban Region to see her. After they expressed their shock and disbelief, they had one thing in common: the naevi had to be removed as quickly as possible. One plastic surgeon had a drastic solution. He suggested a tangential shaving to be done immediately. There was a possibility that the naevi had not penetrated all the layers of skin by the age of six weeks. By shaving the naevi off, layer after layer, they hoped that they would discover a layer of unaffected skin - a long, risky, extensive and painful operation. If successful, it would be the only operation she would ever have to undergo. The team would consist of two senior plastic surgeons working simultaneously, a specialist anaesthetist and a paediatrician.

We had two days to decide. If we decided to go ahead with the operation, it meant that we gave the medical profession the permission to shave off her skin. If we decided against the operation the threat of malignant melanoma together with the gross disfiguration and the agonizing discomfort would hang over our heads. We did not know what to do, however, we really had no choice. We prayed, decided to give consent and took the chance.

On Monday, 24 October 1988, I carried my six-week-old baby into the hospital theatre and gave her to the theatre nurse. Resje knew what was about to happen. She knew she had to drink from this cup. I stood watching her, not being able to drink for her. She did not cry. She was wide-awake. She looked into my eyes.

I wondered why God did not send His legions of angels to come and help His Son, Jesus, when the soldiers tortured Him. Could He not come up with another plan to save mankind? I had to stand there and watch. I could not do anything. She was my lamb that I carried into the butcher's den. She needed to be slain for my sin, her father's sin and the sin of our ancestors.

I had read enough about Abraham, the father of faith, to realize that I was not Abraham. The little bit of faith that I had when she was born, disappeared. The Shunammite woman did not have to fight for her child for six weeks without sleep. She only had to hold fast to her faith for one day. I had no strength and was exhausted from lack of sleep, trying to cope with the shock and pain of her suffering.

Looking at the tumours, hearing the repeated refusals of doctors to become involved and living under the curse of God brought me to a valley of death that I had to go through - I was exhausted.

I tried to remember how her eyes looked immediately after she was born. Life was in them. However, what I had been seeing for the last six weeks was exactly the opposite. I saw only death, torment, agony, suffering, no hope, nor any future. I wanted to stab out my own eyes and walk in circles as the blinded Samson did.

Jesus had touched me on my hospital bed, yes, but where was He now?

During the four and a half-hour operation the two plastic surgeons shaved off all the affected skin. The effect on her body was similar to being burnt extensively with boiling water. When she came out of the hospital theatre, you could not distinguish between the colours of her lips and chin. She was pale, deathly cold, barely breathing. For almost two months after the operation, she was confined to an incubator, isolated in a sterile room and treated as an extensively burnt patient. She was in bandages from her head to her toes. There was not a part of her body where I could touch her without hurting her. Every time I had to breastfeed her, I had to pick her up out of the incubator resting her on a soft pillow. She screamed so much that by the second day after the operation her voice was hoarse. On the third day, she lost her voice completely. That did not prevent her from screaming. She carried on. Silent screams. She screamed with an open mouth with full lungs, yet with no sound coming out.

The doctor came to change her dressings daily. I stood there, watching how they took her through hell and back. The dressings stuck to her raw flesh. The doctor had to tear and pull them loose, taking raw flesh with them. Then he put her in a salt bath, cleaned the wounds and redid the dressings. She was on a torture rack, the doctor being her torturer. She had to live through excruciating torment. Flashes have been branded into my memory - the agonizing pain on her little face, the open silent mouth, raw flesh.

On Tuesday, 1 November, a week after the operation, she developed a dreaded infection. Within 24 hours, every wound on her body became septic. The foul smell was unbearable.

Patients and visitors in the adjoining rooms were repulsed by it, even the medical staff had to fight off their nausea.

Resje, who carried life within her, became a rotten piece of raw meat with an open hole for a mouth. She desperately wanted to be near me, to feel my touch. She yearned for my breast of life-giving, soothing, milk. I held her on the pillow, with her mouth over my breast, my face buried in the sepsis of her wounds. I smelled how death was devouring us both.

I could not understand why she craved something from me to sustain her, as I carried no life in me. I became rotten within. Each wound on her body tore my soul into pieces. She could not make a sound, neither could I.

I did not want daily life to go on as usual. I wanted life to come to a standstill. People walked past me, busy with their daily routines, not even realizing that my baby was rotting away. Cars passed me on their way to nowhere. People looked past me. I tried to tell people. I stopped strangers in the street, telling them about my baby, but they thought I was mad. I learned quickly it is one thing to suffer; it is another thing to show the world your suffering. People close to me tried to speak about other topics, like the weather and politics, to try to take my mind off my dying baby. Christians folded their hands and said that they would pray for us. They prayed for us in their quiet times where we could not see or hear their prayers. I learned to become quiet. I learned to smile and to say she is doing well. I put a mask on and I knew how other people looked behind their masks. Every dark night I took my mask off and I looked in the mirror of my soul and saw my nakedness and loneliness.

The only way I could convince everybody that I could handle Resje's suffering was to pretend that I could handle it. I put a Christian smile on my face and tried to convince everybody about the goodness of the Lord. I listened to empty words of how God has sent His angels to carry us where we can no longer walk, so that if we look carefully now we will find only one set of footprints in the sand. I listened to the techniques people described of how to steal back our joy that the devil has stolen from us. I read about a God who wants to bless us with prosperity and all the good things of life.

I chose to go the route of curses and blessings. Friends gave us tapes and books about curses and blessings by Derek Prince. We worked through them, studied and meditated on them. Pastors and Christian leaders confirmed that this was a curse from God. I started with my sins, confessing every known and unknown sin that I had ever done in my life, consciously and unconsciously, from conception, while I was in my mother's womb to my present life. I not only confessed it, I renounced it and I repented from it. Then I went on to my mother's sin. I confessed and renounced on her behalf every known and unknown sin that she had ever done in her life, consciously and unconsciously, from her birth date to the present. Then I went to her parents and to her mother's grandparents and her father's grandparents, going back four generations. Then I went on to my father's sin and his forefathers. We did the same with Charl and his forefathers.

Our four parents were alive when Resje was born. All four of them believed in Jesus Christ. They were active Christians who went to church every Sunday. We told them about the blessings and curses. They started repenting with us. We called forth all our generational sins and curses. We called forth all the curses that could have been spoken over us. We renounced them. I begged on my knees for weeks - confessing, renouncing, repenting, and seeking God's forgiveness. After we put all the possible curses that could have been on our ancestors and us on the cross of Jesus, we asked God to turn them into blessings. We turned to all the open doors that gave the devil the legal right to enter into our family and we closed them. We went for deliverance ministry and healing. We anointed Resje's clothing. We chased out all the demonic forces in our house and lives. We burned all the books that were offensive to God. We destroyed everything in our house that we thought was not an example of a Christian home. We began praying, attending Bible studies and prayer meetings. We started reading and studying the Bible, tithing, listening to praise and worship music.

We turned our backs on our past way of life and turned towards God. It was not difficult for our new lifestyle to adjust to this drastic change. The circumstances were of such a nature that we could not carry on with the way we lived before Resje's birth. Our new way of life was simply an adaptation to new circumstances.

I grabbed at God with both arms, with my heart and with my intellect. I thought now that we were cleansed and delivered from all curses, we were in a position to receive Jesus' forgiveness and to come into God's presence. I begged Him for a miracle. I acknowledged Him as the Almighty Lord who created heaven and earth. He is love. He will never permit the curse of a previous dispensation to influence His loving child in the future. He will make an end to all this. He gave people the wisdom and the ability to cut out the evil curse in a six-week-old-body.

I could not understand why He chose such a painful method for her healing, but maybe He had to go to that length to get my attention. I accepted His choice of healing. I knew that as soon as the wind and the sea would become calm, Resje's tumours would be gone and her suffering would be over.

My faith grew. I knew God had forgiven me. I felt like Abraham. I had enough faith to move mountains. I waited for Him to speak. I knew He only had to speak to heal her. The doctors do their part; God does the healing. I began praising and thanking God for her healing, proclaiming it. This dying, rotting baby was not too difficult for God to heal. He was going to give her a new healthy skin. He was going to remake her skin, recreating her. She would have a beautiful, perfect skin. I could not stop praising Him. I honoured Him, thanked Him. Hallelujah.

I fed my baby with the rotten smell of death in my nostrils but with a heart filled with joy and anticipation. I could not wait for her skin to heal. Every day, when the doctor removed her dressing, I stood on tiptoes, ready to burst out in laughter and excitement for the miracle that God was going to perform in our midst. We took photographs of her skin the night before the operation. I held onto them. I thought the whole world would be touched when they see this mighty miracle of God when He healed her skin.

The purpose for my baby's suffering was obvious. God wanted to change my heart towards Him. Through her suffering, He had done it. She led me to the living God. I began praising Him for Resje's suffering. He brought life to me through my baby girl. I could not thank Him enough.

He answered me through a singular verse:
> "Be still, and know that I am God; I will be exalted among the nations, I will be exalted in the earth!"
> (Psalm 46:10, NKJ)

Peace, that goes beyond all human understanding filled my heart. My thoughts became quiet. I believed with all my heart that God forgave our sins, that He removed the curse(s) and that He wanted to bless us with Resje's healing. I believed this was going to be a great miracle, albeit through the hands of the surgeons. My duty was to make sure that He would get the glory and I was determined that He would.

The anticipated miracle carried me through the days and nights. My heart worked overtime. I praised and thanked Him. I felt so small and insignificant and could not understand why God had chosen us to perform one of His greatest miracles. I looked at her a thousand times a day and saw how healthy, normal skin was growing underneath the dressings. God had chosen Resje to suffer for a short time so that He could crown her with honour and favour.

I pronounced her healing, preparing everyone for the miracle. I waited upon God, watching her skin with the eyes of an eagle. I began connecting with other people who were suffering too. I visited other children in the hospital, reaching out to their parents. A new hope came into my eyes and my footsteps felt as light as a feather.

Then came the devastating blow.

Six weeks after the operation as her skin started healing, every thick, life-threatening, pitch-black naevus returned. The operation had been a complete failure. Her time in hell had no purpose. There was no miracle. There was no blessing. God turned His back on my child and on me.

As I ran blindly out of the hospital, I relived my seventh birthday. I had a splinter underneath my thumbnail and my parents could not get it out. They took me to the hospital in my party dress. The doctor was old and harsh. He had no time for the hysterics of a seven-year-old. Without an injection or trying to calm me, he grabbed my hand and started peeling off my nail with a scalpel. I remember how I tried to pull away screaming at him to stop. I screamed that I would pray to dear Lord Jesus and that He would take out the splinter. The doctor put his surly face in front of me and screamed back: "You keep quiet now! Dear Lord Jesus is not here. I am".

In 1 Samuel 4 we read that in battle, at a place called Ebenezer, Israel was unexpectedly defeated by the Philistines. The ark of the covenant of the Lord was in Shiloh. The ark had a special meaning to the Israelites because that was the place of the glorious presence of God. They decided to go and fetch the ark of the Lord. To bring the ark into their camp was as good as if the Living God came into their camp. They shouted so loudly when the ark came into the camp that the earth shook. That put fear into the Philistines. Even the Philistines believed that the mighty God of the Israelites, who struck the Egyptians with all the plagues in the wilderness, was now fighting for the Israelites - they were doomed.

Full in the confidence of their God, the Israelites attacked the Philistines. However, that was the day that God turned His back on His people. Thirty thousand infantry soldiers died. The Israelites were defeated again and had to flee to their tents. The ark of God was captured and the two sons of Eli, the priest, were killed. When Eli heard the devastating news, he fell backwards and died. The wife of his son, Phinehas, was about to give birth. When she heard the shocking news of Israel's defeat, the death of her husband and her father-in-law and the capture of the ark, her labour pains came upon her. She gave birth to a boy. Then she named him Ichabod, which means that the glory of God has departed from Israel.

How do you hold onto a God who has turned His back on you? You know He is there somewhere, because you came close to Him. I went to fetch the Ark of the Covenant in Shiloh; I also gave a triumphant shout of victory when I found it. I believed, like the Israelites, He was going to fight for us. All my confidence was in Him. For some reason, God looked at Resje and named her Ichabod.

Looking around me I saw a world of suffering. Humanity was broken and beaten. People who did not suffer physically, suffered emotionally, or spiritually, or mentally, or financially, or relationally. I could not find the love, joy, peace and patience of the Bible in the eyes of people, particularly Christians. Fear, anger and sadness filled their eyes. I knew about the bitterness, the loneliness and the hurt in their hearts.

People around me were fighting, divorcing and dying. People had problems with their finances, emotions and children, some trying to escape from reality through food, alcohol and drugs. The suffering was ongoing and never-ending.

People stared at Resje in shock and horror. We were the marked ones, the scapegoats of society, the outcasts. I felt guilty, vulnerable, naked, unloved and rejected by God. I was not one of His favourites and He had no compassion on me and my little baby girl. She did not deserve to be born like this. God chased Resje out into the desert, deserting her there and by doing it, punished me by not chasing me out into the desert. Everyone could see the banality of this.

I could no longer look people in the eyes. On the one hand, I felt shameful. On the other, I sensed their hidden hurt and pain. I was afraid that our hurt would cleave open their hearts, afraid that my eyes would expose their nakedness. I did not want to look upon any more suffering.

I realized that the world was full of broken people – everyone with hurt, stains and tumours, trying to survive.

People who suffered most were Christians. The non-Christians showed their pain and anger to anyone who showed enough interest. They had worldly escape routes. Their friends helped them, encouraged them, drank with them, got angry with them and escaped with them.

However, I discovered that many Christians feel guilty for not living in the Garden of Eden anymore. Because we feel guilty, we hide our pain from the rest of the world, pretending everything is fine. We proclaim a gracious God who wants us to have enough faith in Him so that He can swing His magic wand and create a better world for all. If we only believe, then all things are possible. It is our own fault that we are in this mess, because we do not have enough faith. We only have to persevere, because every cloud has a silver lining.

We create a false Utopia and in this false world, we dare not show anyone our suffering. We create a superhuman race with a super God who can do anything, in a sense similar to Hitler's philosophy. Any imperfection not fitting into society is sent to the gas chambers. This leads to people hiding their inner pain. If you dare expose your pain to somebody else, you put this brother or sister in an awkward situation: Firstly by reminding you of your own vulnerability and secondly, not knowing how to handle other people's suffering in a world where we say Jesus is the answer.

We need to come to the place where we have to face the reality that in this sense we as Christians reflect a sick, false world full of lies.

I started asking question upon question. Why do we live? What is the meaning of life? Why can God not take us away to His Heavenly Paradise where the streets are made of gold with no room for hospitals? Why does God choose to bring suffering onto this person and not the next? Does God bring suffering? If He does not, why does He not end it? I asked questions until I had no more questions to ask, not finding any answers.

In my heart a huge filing system developed - one filing cabinet containing the disappointments, another rejection. The third cabinet was for the pain I could handle, the fourth for the pain I could not. The storeroom carpets were made of mohair of incomprehensibility, the walls painted with the colours of helplessness and powerlessness, the ceiling was made of wood of dismay and the name of the key that fitted into the lock was disillusionment.

God could not be found anywhere in that storeroom. He was sitting high up in heaven. I thought He had come down to heal and forgive us, but He only briefly came down to take His glory away from us. I looked up one more time, but all I could see was the cup filled to overflowing that God held out to us. Unlike Judas, I did not betray Him. I did not turn my back on Him. He left us.

In 2 Kings 23, we read how Josiah, king of Judah, reacted when he read the Book of the Law. During the reign of his father, Amon, and his grandfather, Manasseh, they did evil in the eyes of God. Josiah repented, correcting everything. He renewed the Covenant with the Lord; removed from the temple all the articles made for idols, burning it outside the walls of Jerusalem. He slaughtered the pagan priests, tore down the quarters of the male shrine prostitutes, pulled down the altars the kings of Judah had erected, smashed all the sacred stones, got rid of the spirit mediums, household gods, idols and all other detestable things seen in Judah and Jerusalem. He did everything that was right in the eyes of the Lord.

Verse 25 says this about King Josiah:

> "Now before him there was no king like him, who turned to the Lord with all his heart, with all his soul, and with all his might, according to all the Law of Moses; nor after him did any arise like him." (NKJ)

In verses 26 and 27 we read about how God reacted towards this godly son of His:

> "Nevertheless the Lord did not turn from the fierceness of His great wrath, with which His anger was aroused against Judah, because of all the provocations with which Manasseh had provoked Him. And the Lord said, 'I will also remove Judah from My sight, as I have removed Israel, and will cast

off this city Jerusalem which I have chosen, and the house of which I said, My name shall be there.'" (NKJ)

How can anyone understand God? I knew His ways are not our ways, but if God was not merciful against Josiah after everything Josiah did for God, how could I expect God to be merciful towards us?

I had to find help. To exist and to carry on with life, I had to turn to somebody or something. Someone stronger than me, had to take care of me. I did not want to escape from reality with alcohol or drugs, pills or food. I wanted to stay as sane as possible. Pastors, teachers and apostles could not bring me the healing balm of Gilead. Others were just as broken and confused as I was.

Because I repelled a strong and mighty King, a Father who gladly gave up His Son, I had no choice but to turn to a slain, broken, tortured lamb. I turned to my little slain lamb. I turned to Resje. She was only a baby, yet her spirit was stronger than mine.

Culture is a learned thing. People who suffer go into survival mode. When in survival mode, the laws of nature take over. The bare necessities of life, the basics, become important. You have to become strong and fit, because it is only the fittest that survive in this broken world.

My desire for Resje to survive and to escape from the hell she was living in, became stronger than all else. I knew that in this world it is possible for a mother to pick up a vehicle if her child is caught under it. I decided to lift up my baby, to become so strong that the whole world would see me holding her high. She needed to be strong to one day share her secret of life with me. She would need to cleave open the Rock to give me water. If I died in the process, she would have to be strong enough to roll away the stone from my grave.

Together with mother's milk, I gave her a fighting spirit, a spirit of courage and of endurance. I taught her how to have an attitude of perseverance, how to get up and go after repeated falls. In later years, I taught her how to love and to laugh while her body was screaming out in agony. I taught her how to verbally express her feelings, how to smile at people and look deep into their hearts. These qualities had to become part of her personality, her character traits.

We went looking for a medical doctor who could help us. We could not find anyone who wanted to take her on as a patient. We were a problem case, a statistic. The doctors were full of excuses, shrugging their shoulders, turning away to the next patient. I contacted a magazine in South Africa who published her story. She was eight months by then. After the article was published, a woman phoned me to give me details of her son's plastic surgeon. We flew to Pretoria (about 600 km from Durban), saw the doctor who became not only her plastic surgeon, but also a friend and saviour for the next fourteen years of her life, performing sixty-six of her seventy-four operations.

I became strong with her. I had to carry her physically as well as emotionally. I accepted a lecturing post at the University of Natal. I took Resje to a crèche for a few hours each day, while I lectured to hundreds of students. I went to work after two hours sleep every night. It was impossible, but I knew a mother could lift up a car if her child was under it. For my child I could do the impossible. And when it became physically impossible for me to carry on, I had my husband, Charl, to help me. He helped putting her to sleep, bathing her, dressing her, singing to her, staying up with her.

I was an outstanding lecturer. My students and colleagues never knew about my lack of sleep. We totally got lost in our studies for a few hours each day. After a day's lecturing, Resje occupied the rest. She sat on my lap with only a nappy on while I rubbed her back with a soft cloth. The rubbing did not take the irritation away nor did it bring any relief. It served to calm her. That was all I could do. I tried to soothe my hysterical child. I never succeeded, but I never stopped trying.

It was impossible to have a normal conversation. Everyone stared at the child in agony on my lap. I became a robot with arms that had to move up and down, because that was all she wanted. There was no joy or satisfaction in my motherhood. Her primary need was not milk, food, or dry nappies. It was to get rid of the pain. I could give her milk and food and change her nappies, but I could not fulfill her primary need. I felt helpless.

The days and nights turned to weeks, the weeks to months, the months to years, and the years became our existence. Somewhere along this route, I accepted that suffering was part of our lives. It was not that I became used to Resje's skin condition - it was simply part of life. Our daily life consisted of little sleep and much suffering.

I could not understand God. To me He was not consistent. I was greatly disturbed with God. I was perplexed and felt rejected. He says He is a God of love, but He appears not to be involved in a world of suffering. I can understand why there are so many atheists and agnostics. People, like me, who are disappointed in a God who does not want to become involved, cannot believe He exists. The only true thing that people want is to have a little place in the sun. However, if God exists, and created the sun as Christians believe, then He wants to take the sun all for Himself. Surely then, it is better for your own sanity to believe that there is no God. If people cannot exist the way they want to exist, then they create a God who does not exist.

I could not escape so easily. After Resje's birth, I had a personal experience with a living God. To make matters worse, He touched me, not only through her eyes, but also on the way to the private ward. To me, He existed. He was a reality. He only did not care. My struggle was never a simplistic seeking whether God existed or not, my struggle became a complicated, philosophical search for the reasons behind God's withdrawal in a world of suffering.

When God sent His Son to earth, Jesus became involved in a healing ministry. Jesus expressed His desire to heal the sick and the disabled. He became the heavenly doctor who cured the incurable, healed the impossible and touched the untouchables.

The New Testament Jesus was involved with people – He healed and delivered, raising them from the dead. When Jesus saw the man with the infirmity at the pool of Bethesda, who had unsuccessfully waited at the water's edge for thirty-eight years, He immediately had compassion on him and healed him. When they brought the blind, the lame and the paralyzed to Jesus, He touched and healed them. When they brought the lepers to Him, He cured them. He came for the sick, for us. We were sick. We needed a doctor. Jesus came down to earth, specifically for us and for others like us. I stretched out my hand for Him to heal us, but something stopped Him in His tracks. This was not the Jesus we read of in the New Testament.

I could not understand this. God was not the same yesterday, today and tomorrow. This implied His Word was not true. I struggled with two options. The first was to believe that God could not heal Giant Pigmented Naevi. He cried with us, but He could not heal her. To think of a God who wanted to heal her but could not, brought about a strange comfort. I viewed Him as a God with limitations and for a little while He became quite human to me. However, in observing the world of suffering, I concluded that God could not heal the blind, lame, deaf, mute, intellectually disabled and everyone else in need of healing. Such a God was hopeless and powerless.

The second option was to view God as a Holy Being, a Creator, positioned in heaven. He gave us everything we needed. He gave us intellectual powers to reason, the ability to work and earn money, wisdom and knowledge to attain technical and professional qualifications. We had to fend for ourselves, to get out, get a job and money to provide for our families. We had to search for medical help, accepting their fallibility. Medical incompetence acquits God.

God created the universe, stood back and saw how mankind ruined it, not interfering.

He was there, He existed, but He did not become personally involved. He was like a puppet master who pulled selected strings. People got lucky when He pulled their string while under medical treatment, or they received a financial windfall on the death of a relative. Of the puppets I knew very few had strings pulled. You could get angry with God, or try to ignore Him. You could beg Him to pull a string until you were blue in the face. He was the Creator, the Potter - you were merely the clay, the creation that dared not question the Creator.

This second option gave my flesh great satisfaction, because I could vent all my anger on God. However, the Bible does not substantiate or verify this view. The God who is portrayed in the Bible is a God who came down to have fellowship with His children. Yes, often becoming angered by His children, but never indifferent. He came down to talk to Moses in the burning bush. He came down as a cloud and a fire to protect the Israelites on their journey to the Promised Land. He called to the boy Samuel in an audible voice. He spoke to the prophets; He commanded the whale to spit Jonah out of his mouth. He sent His angels to inform Zacharias and Elizabeth, Joseph and Mary that their boys were chosen. A study of Jesus confirms this view. Jesus was everywhere and got involved with everyone. The Bible portrays God as a loving, concerning, caring, miracle-working God.

Because of all the suffering I saw around me, my first option was not sound. To adapt to my second option, I realized that I had to stop reading the Bible. The Bible portrayed a different God. This would mean that I had something in common with atheists. Atheists denied the existence of God. I had to deny the existence of the Bible. To me this was not an acceptable option.

I read about Jacob's struggle with God at Jabbok. God could not overcome Jacob, so God put out the socket of Jacob's hip and Jacob limped for the rest of his life. I knew I was not the most intelligent girl in the world, but I regarded my intellect as one of my strongest assets. It felt as if God could not prevail against my reasoning, therefore He struck my mind and emotions, as He did with Jacob's hip. It felt as if I had a limp in my reasoning and emotions. My mind and heart struggled with God. I could not understand Him and He could not overcome me. If it were not for Genesis 32, I would have given up many times. In His struggle with Jacob, God pleaded with Jacob to let Him go for the day was breaking, and then Jacob said:

> "... I will not let You go unless You bless me!"
> (Genesis 32:26, NKJ)

Even though Jacob was stronger than God, he understood that God could bless Him. It was the same for me. In my search for answers, God could not provide me with a satisfying one, but deep within I knew He was the One who could bless me. The blessing that God gave Jacob was very interesting. The blessing was to change Jacob's name to Israel, thus transforming Jacob's character from deceiver to a prince of God.

I was more interested in the reason for the blessing. God states in Genesis 3: 28:

> "Your name shall no longer be called Jacob, but Israel; for you have struggled with God and with men, and have prevailed." (NKJ)

To me, the answer was with God. In front of me stretched a huge mountain. I had to get over it, everything pointed to this mountain. I was on the right track. God had the answer. I had to keep up the struggle, to prevail like Jacob in my struggle against God. I feared that I might not have the strength or that I might capitulate; yet I knew without doubt that God existed. He wanted to heal Resje and to be involved. My mission was to continue searching the reasons preventing God's intervention. That was my struggle with God. I needed to prevail for God to change my identity and not to only bless me, but particularly my daughter.

The first two years after Resje's birth was a ferocious walk with God. I concluded that I had to do something before God would touch Resje. Whenever I thought that I had not asked enough forgiveness, I would repeatedly beg God to forgive my sins. Whenever I thought that I had not confessed all the sins of my forefathers, I would again confess, repent, renounce and ask God's forgiveness. I was certain there were hidden sins somewhere in our lives. I kept repenting the hidden sins of my ancestors. We took Resje to faith healers and faith services whenever the opportunity presented itself. They all prayed for her. They broke off curses, confessing God's blessings over her.

I felt guilty that I did not have the time or energy to do something for God. The hope remained that when Resje allowed me some time, I would start doing things for Him – visiting people in hospitals, prisons, the widows and orphans, baking for the poor and the hungry, begin a crèche. Then, I thought, it would be possible to show God that I was no longer jealous of babies with normal skin.

In the last chapter of the last book of the Bible Jesus says He is coming back soon and He is bringing with Him the reward to give to everyone according to his work. I reasoned that had to be the last thing to do. I could not physically do anything for God, so I begged Him for forgiveness that I was too busy with Resje and too tired to hear from Him what He wanted me to do.

I realized I had to get rid of any bitterness in my heart. Forgiveness was the next phase. I forgave my husband, parents and my ancestors for their sins, the two plastic surgeons for the unsuccessful operation and God for not being involved with us. I concluded there must be a reason, so I forgave Him. I forgave myself for not being able to touch God's heart to heal my child. Lastly, I forgave Resje for taking up my energy and time, preventing me from working for God and His Kingdom. It was not easy to forgive. It was a long deliberate process.

Slowly I changed. I could not find anything funny enough to laugh about anymore or a topic worth discussing. I stopped asking questions, it felt as if I had asked all the questions in the world. Gradually my tears and hope faded. A stillness and emptiness filled my life. Days were filled, sitting on a chair with Resje, stroking her back, staring at the naevi, hearing her pain and seeing her agony.

I remembered the Parable of the Good Samaritan. After Resje was born, the two of us were on our way from Jerusalem to Jericho. We had a destination that we had to reach - to discover the Life within her. We had clothes on our body - an identity. I felt special because I thought God chose us to reveal His glory. God's Word was food to still my hunger and to keep me strong.

Thieves caught us on the way, stripping us of our clothing, food and destination. That was not enough for them. They wounded, tormented and burnt us with hot water. They left us for dead. We screamed until we lost our voices. Nobody came to our assistance. The Priest and the Levite passed us by on the other side, because of our revolting, rotten smell.

I searched for a God who could take the pain and suffering away, a God who could answer our prayers with a miracle, a God who could bless and prosper us with earthly peace. I yearned for a God who could carry us when we could not walk anymore. I longed for the God of the universe, the Lion of Judah, the King of kings and Lord of lords, the Mighty One. This God turned His back on us, exactly like the Priest and the Levite. As God did with king Josiah, He did not turn away from the heat of his fierce anger, which burnt against Resje.

Isaiah 53: 2-5 expressed my thoughts:

> *My daughter, Resje, there is no beauty that we should desire you. You are despised and rejected by men, a child of sorrows and acquainted with grief. We hid our faces from you. Surely, you have borne our griefs and carried our sorrows; yet, we esteem you stricken, smitten by God, and afflicted. You were wounded for our transgressions. You were bruised for our iniquities...*

Somewhere, on a street-corner, a Samaritan stood. He was not a mighty God; He was not the Lion of Judah. Because he was a Samaritan, he was filth to the Jews. He was a slain, broken Lamb, covered in open bleeding wounds. He had oil, wine and bandages in His pockets. His name was Jesus. He lifted the oil. I looked Him in the eye. I knew a different God, high and mighty, indifferent to suffering. To me, this stranger was but a broken Samaritan. I refused His oil, wine and bandages.

I held on to my baby and turned away.

Chapter Four

THE CHOSEN ONE

Saul of Tarsus was a persecutor of the followers of Jesus Christ. On the road to Damascus God appeared to him and struck him with blindness. God then called a man by the name of Ananias to go and pray for Saul in order for God to restore Saul's blindness. Ananias feared Saul, afraid that he might have him arrested.

In Acts 9:15-16 (NKJ), we read the Lord's answer to Ananias:

> "Go, for he is a chosen vessel of Mine to bear My name before Gentiles, kings, and the children of Israel. For I will show him how many things he must suffer for My name's sake."

The plastic surgeon in Pretoria immediately started with plastic surgery procedures under general anaesthetics. Resje was eight months old. During the next three years he operated on her monthly. He concentrated on her legs, buttocks and head. The process was long and painful – every naevus had to be excised, little by little. One of the tumours on her leg required fourteen separate operations to completion. She developed infection after almost every operation. Often the infection was so severe that the wounds tore open. This required going back to Pretoria from Durban - a distance of six hundred kilometers. The surgeon then had to remove the infected flesh and re-stitch the wound under general anaesthetics. It was common for her to be on three to four courses of antibiotics after each operation. After one particular operation, she required five courses of antibiotics. For the first three years, her legs were put in plaster casts for three out of four weeks in every month. While other babies crawled and discovered the world, Resje sat on my lap with stiff legs and cried.

Her fear for doctors and hospitals changed every visit into a nightmare. To lessen the trauma, she was usually discharged on the same day. My father and mother lived in a town 70 kilometers from the hospital. This served as a recovery point, set in a loving family atmosphere with doting grandparents and close enough to the hospital for emergencies. I had to learn how to dress Resje's wounds and how to clean infected areas as big as the palm of my hand without fainting. I was permitted to carry her into the operating theatre and to administer the gas mask over her mouth for each operation, because she would not let anyone else touch her.

She had to learn how to handle the staring faces, shock, disgust, and the blatancy of people's inquisitive nature, many questions and rejection. We did not know what was worse - people who asked what was going on or people who ignored her. It was difficult for her to accept that in order to prevent the stitches from tearing, she could not run like other children. The specialist used stainless steel clips that looked like staples on her. She had between 100 and 150 clips after each operation. For medical reasons it was important for her not to become too dependent on painkillers, therefore she had to learn to cope without strong medication. She found it very hard to accept that she was different to other children; she could not dress the way other little girls dressed or do what other children did. It was extremely hard for her to accept her disability.

There were no sweat pores on the naevi, meaning that her skin had no cooling mechanism. Durban has a hot tropical climate. The heat aggravated the skin irritation. Once she was hot, it took hours to cool her. She was not allowed to go into the sun because the sun's ultra-violet rays were extremely dangerous to her as it could produce cancerous cells.

I often thought she was going to lose her sound mind because of the unbearable irritation. The first words she said were not "daddy" or "mommy", but "eina" (ouch) and "help". The word "help" became a swear word to me. She extended this to: "Help, Mommy", and then later to: "Help me, Mommy!"

Her struggle with pain peaked at night. The struggle to find relief tore my heart in two. All I could do was to rub her back and try to keep her hands away from scratching the naevi. I tried to relax her by singing and praying to God. I tried to keep my voice as calm as possible, while my soul was screaming away in agony. Once awake, it took hours before she was overcome by exhaustion and drifted into a restless sleep again.

Then came her questions in a screaming voice bordering madness: "Why me? Why can't God take this away? Why can't I be free from this? What is happening to me?" She looked at me for answers I did not have.

By January 1992, at the age of three, she had already had thirty operations. The surgeon needed to have substantial donor areas of "clean" skin for skin transplants before concentrating on the large naevus on her back. The process was substantially aggravated by the formation of keloids – thick scar tissue that formed on the site of almost every excision. The only consolation was that each operation removed a percentage of the potential life-threatening tumours, the disadvantage being scars itching almost as badly as the naevi.

In addition, the scars were there to remind me every day of the hell Resje was going through.

During the remainder of 1992 and 1993, fourteen operations using a method of stretching the skin by using implanted expanders under the skin, were attempted. The idea was that the stretched skin would then be used to cover the adjoining excised areas. Unfortunately with each expander infection developed. The stretched skin intended for the naevi was then needed to cover the gaping openings caused by the infections. By the end of 1993, the doctor discarded this method, not gaining one millimetre of skin.

Whilst other four year olds climbed about, ran and played, Resje was either in the hospital or at home in an uncomfortable position with draining tubes, begging for pain relief.

The surgeon's eyes often showed his disappointment with her healing. She was, indeed, a unique case. None of his other patients struggled this much. However, he read our desperate eyes, knowing that we would find no one else to operate. He never said a discouraging word and knew he was our only hope.

Although Resje was immensely fearful of hospitals and the operations, the surgeon became her hero. She called him "oom Koos" (uncle Koos). He called her "my meisie" (my girl). Whenever she hurt a finger or a toe at home, she would ask me to take her to "oom Koos". He would know what to do. Whenever she had a cold or a cough, she begged me to make an appointment with her plastic surgeon, because oom Koos would fix this cough. She believed in him the way a little child believes in Santa Claus.

At the age of five, she once asked me if I understood her pain and when I turned with tears towards her, she grabbed my arms, looked me in the eye and answered: "No mummy, you don't know the pain I have. Oom Koos, Jesus and I know, but you don't know."

When she was seven years old, she wanted her ears pierced but she had no desire to willingly subject herself to more pain. She asked oom Koos. Painlessly, while she was under general anaesthetics, the plastic surgeon removed some of the deadly naevi and then pierced her ears for her.

At the hospital before an operation, she would run into the arms of her plastic surgeon, he would pick her up and the two of them would hug like old friends. One day, he turned his back on me holding her in his arms, his face buried in her neck. I walked around the two of them wanting to make eye contact with him, only to see tears rolling down his face.

From the very first appointment to sixty-six operations later, he was never only her doctor. He was much more. He was her "uncle Koos", a friend, a hero and a helper. He understood her fears, her pain and her dreams. To him, she was much more than simply a patient - she was his girl.

On 22 November 1994, during Resje's forty-eighth operation, the surgeon did a skin graft on her back. During a three-hour operation, he removed the extensive naevus that covered her back. Donor skin was taken from her thighs, initially from the back part of her legs. It was a full thickness skin graft, meaning he needed all the layers of skin from the donor area, leaving it completely raw. He then removed the naevus, section at a time, immediately grafting strips of skin from her legs onto the excised sites.

The extent of the excisions demanded more donor skin than the back of her thighs could deliver. Her calves were unsuitable due to extensive scarring from previous operations. Her position on the operating table could not be altered for fear of dislodging the fresh transplants. Consequently, her legs were pulled off the theatre table until the front of her thighs were exposed. The surgeon then kneeling under the operating table removed donor skin from the upper parts of both thighs. He succeeded in getting enough skin to remove the entire naevus from her back. Twenty patches of donor skin and over 500 stainless steel clips covered the area previously occupied by the naevus. Her back resembled a quilt, consisting of live skin – not material.

This particular operation was extremely traumatic for her; nevertheless, in one operation the surgeon removed the black and the pain, the itching and the agony, death and hell that were on her back and neck.

The donor area was more painful than the skin graft on her back. She was covered in thick dressings from her neck down to her knees, and was not able to walk. Because of the extensive loss of blood, blood transfusions were necessary. She also required intravenous drips and a catheter was inserted. She begged me to take her to my parents' home for recovery there. One of the nurses told her that they would not discharge her unless she was able to walk.

The urge to survive became stronger than the excruciating pain. A determination filled her eyes. She was adamant that she would walk.

Three days after the operation she lifted herself off the bed with supernatural strength. I had to help wheel the pole with the blood supply, the drip and the catheter. With the 500 clips on her back and raw legs, she managed to walk a few steps.

She screamed out in a delirious voice: "Do you see, Mom, I am walking! I am walking! I am walking!"

My soul shook and my heart screamed out with her. I could not scream at my mother, I screamed at God. "Do You see? We are walking! We are still alive. My broken child is still alive! She is walking! She has survived another operation. She has made it! She lives! She is alive!"

For me to survive I had to find the meaning of Resje's suffering. I know in this life we only know in part and one day we will know in full, however, I could not accept that what was happening to her was something unfortunate or simply part of life without any meaning. I had to find the truth behind this. Like Jacob, I had to wrestle with God, until I found if not all, a partial explanation.

In the Bible, Thomas, who incidentally later became doubting Thomas, was also looking for an element of clarity in this confused life. Jesus answered Thomas by saying to him:

> "I am the way, the truth, and the life. No one comes to the Father except through Me." (John 14:6, NKJ)

Now I wish I could say to all the believers who are reading my story how easy it was for me to look for the truth and because Jesus is the truth, I stumbled onto Jesus one day and from that day on my life has never been the same. Unfortunately, this has not been as easy for me.

I have always believed in Jesus. I believed and confessed that He was the truth, the way and the life. I even knew He was real. My struggle was where was He in all this suffering and why was He not helping us. This skin condition was a curse to me and I was angry with God for not turning this curse into a blessing. I could not understand why He ignored us. We were

His children, we accepted Him as our Lord and Saviour, yet He did not help us.

I had to meet Him face to face, to look at truth through my own eyes, not finding Him through the comforting and encouraging words of friends, family and pastors. They only meant well and I bless them with all my heart that they tried by encouraging us. They only wanted to help and I praise God for brothers and sisters in Christ, nevertheless their encouragement did not bring me into contact with Jesus. I could neither find Him in towns and cities doing miracles, nor in the temple preaching as the Son of God. I could not find the compassionate loving and all-powerful Jesus who performed hundreds of miracles and touched thousands of people.

A starting point had to be found. I went to John 14:6 where Jesus says that no one can come to God the Father except through Him. I realized I had a firm belief in God the Father, the Creator of the Heavens and Earth, sitting in Heaven. In addition to that, I also believed with all my heart that Jesus was the Son of God who died for our sins, for us to live again. I did not deny or hide my anger, I pushed it aside so that my emotions would not interfere in my search.

When Jesus died, the veil of the temple was torn in two and I always thought I had direct access to God through the name of Jesus Christ. Like a magic wand, I waved the name "Jesus Christ" in front of God, whenever I prayed.

Jesus Himself says in Matthew 7:22-23:

> "Many will say to Me in that day, 'Lord, Lord, have we not prophesied in Your name, cast out demons in Your name, and done many wonders in Your name?'

And then I will declare to them, I never knew you…" (NKJ)

I wonder if one day He will turn away all those people who used His name as a magic wand.

I had to throw away the magic wand and had to discard all my preconceived ideas of God the Father, Jesus the Son and the Holy Spirit. I spent over thirty years in the church, reading my Bible, going to Bible studies and prayer meetings without ever seeing Jesus. All I had personally witnessed was a little bit of healing here and there, employment here for somebody, unemployment there for somebody else, rain this season on a neighbour's farm, but no rain the next season. Miraculous healings, television crusades by famous television personalities and Christian books about healing were for others.

The compassionate, all-powerful Jesus Christ was hiding from us. I wanted to find Him and find out why He was hiding from us. I realized I could not go to the Father in the name only of Jesus Christ. His name represents His character. The approach to the Father was in the character of Jesus. That was a different ball game. I had to get to know Jesus. I had to find Him to look upon Him and see Him with my own eyes.

The battle was long and fierce, a struggle between the visible and invisible, the reality of suffering and faith in a God who is good.

My mind and intellect reasoned with God, analyzing Resje's suffering, trying to find meaning in it. I tried to reason with God as a student would approach me, his lecturer, in analyzing a literary work, looking at it from all angles, seeking the true meaning, the theme, motives, setting and characters.

My senses debated with God. I could see Resje's suffering and at the same time stare into God's absence. Her cries echoed in His silence. Simultaneously I was asking, begging and blaming Him. Touching Resje, I felt her broken scars within the emptiness of the air around me, tasting her yearning for help, yet swallowing the bitterness of denial.

My emotions were at war with God: anger, frustration, hatred and tears. When Resje was three years old we moved from Durban to a farm in Zimbabwe. I knew I could not take her to an island isolated from the rest of the world, but at least I could take her out of a sun-filled holiday city with people in their colourful swimming costumes to a remote farm in Africa.

For twelve months, five days a week between 9 and 10 o' clock in the morning, I locked myself in my room and cried. I had no words or plans. I had one hour a day to myself and all I could do was to vent all my anger at God. I expressed it to Him, crying out in bitterness, hating Him, asking, begging and threatening. When I was completely empty, I started crying. I cried until I had no more tears, but still God did not answer me.

It was a bloody battle. I was as bruised and scarred, wounded and hurt as my little girl.

Unlike Jacob who wrestled with God who could not overcome Jacob, God overpowered me. I tried everything to find the answer of God's indifference, and still nothing happened.

Slowly, like a deadly snake, rejection slithered in. I lost all hope, the will to battle on. I still believed in God, but He turned His back on me. I set out to search for the love and goodness of a Heavenly Father, the powerful Son of God who performed miracle after miracle, only to find there was something wrong with us.

Pastors and prophets unknowingly confirmed my rejection. They said: "This skin condition is a curse from God, you have to repent." We repented. "There must be a hidden sin somewhere in your lives." I crept on my knees, confessing the sins of generations upon generations. "You have to have more faith. Just believe!" I prayed and begged for more faith. "Tithe!" We tithed. "Pray!" We prayed. "Give!" We gave, doing everything we were supposed to do. Because there was no response from God, it confirmed to me that God wanted nothing to do with us. We were not His favourites and not chosen by Him, but outcasts.

After each operation, I begged God that Resje would not develop an infection and that the wounds would not tear open. God did the opposite: she developed infections and the wounds tore open. I felt like a dog returning to its own vomit out of hunger because the scraps of food were thrown to the others, beaten and kicked, ignored and refused by my master.

I continued going to church, reading my Bible and praying. I read about God's love, His forgiveness and goodness. However, His promises and words were for other people. I was an outsider, rejected by God. Man and God rejected Resje. We were marked, the scapegoats chased into the desert. God's love, acceptance and healing were reserved for others. I looked at other people, longing to be a sheep in God's camp, but day after day, the gate was shut before we could enter. We were left outside to be devoured by the wolves, not wanted in the sheep paddock. I felt sick and jealous of other people receiving God's love and favour, realizing He did not want to bestow any blessings on us.

People would pass us by, commenting about how they were blessed by God. I wondered what monster existed in us, that God could not bless us the way He blessed others. We were unloved, uncared for and unwanted. For me, this was the pit of hell. In a way, I could understand why God rejected me.

What I could not understand was why He rejected Resje as well.

To make things worse, many people's reactions felt like rejection. They could either not cope with our suffering or did not want to become involved.

I put on a brave smile, went about my daily chores, but deep inside my heart burned with loneliness and the sting of rejection.

There was nothing left in my mind or my soul to give to God. He gave me my intellect to explore Him, but I could not find Him. He gave me my senses but His presence evaded me. I fought Him with the emotions He gave me - with anger, fear, anxiety, bitterness and loneliness and yet He did not appear. I gave Him my time and money; still He kept hiding from me. I wondered if there was another way.

I read in the Bible:

> "… you will seek the Lord your God, and you will find Him if you seek Him with all your heart and with all your soul" (Deuteronomy 4:29, NKJ);

> "And you will seek Me and find Me, when you search for Me with all your heart." (Jeremiah 29:13, NKJ)

I had one thing though that I had not given to God: my heart. My heart was my life. It was sacred to me. It was mine. I was so tortured by Resje's suffering and by rejection that I wanted no one else to see my pain. It was in my heart that I experienced humiliation beyond words, feeling lower than the most disgusting thing on the face of the earth. God always wanted the best of everything. He required a spotless animal for sacrifice, not a maimed one. My heart looked like Resje's back, full of dark stains and blemishes. God wanted something pure and holy, not me, not my heart.

In Job 2:9, Job's wife suggested that Job should curse God and die. She could not accept the horrible God who kept on punishing Job. I certainly felt like this on many occasions. However, Job could not curse God and turn his back on Him, neither could I. Job went so far as to call his wife a foolish woman. I did not want to go down as a foolish woman. If ever I had to go down, God Himself would have to throw me out. I felt like God was in the process of shooting me down, but I knew I had not given Him everything. My heart stood between the two of us. If I gave Him my heart and was shot down, then I would have tried everything. If I did not give Him my heart, I would lose this battle. I had exhausted all my ammunition… except the last: my heart.

How do you give your heart to God?

This was a complicated issue. On the one hand, because I already felt rejected by God, I felt God did not want my heart. However, there was another deep dark side to my hesitation. I confessed my sins to God, knowing that He knew my heart was not pure or holy, a fact that I did not want to accept. To give God my heart meant that I acknowledged I was not pure or holy. My heart was a high and holy place.

Enter another battle – the battle against pride.

I looked into my heart, knowing there were high and mighty emotions of anger and bitterness, underscored by feelings of rejection. I felt justified in having the highs and lows. My pride fell on acknowledging the broken shattered pieces. I could not help my little girl, or myself, nor could I find God. I was poor and broken.

The Book of Revelation describes that no one in heaven or on the earth or under the earth could be found worthy to open the scroll and to loose its seals. John, the author of Revelation started weeping because no one could be found. Then one of the elders turned to John and comforted him saying:

> "… Behold, the Lion of the tribe of Judah, the Root of David, has prevailed to open the scroll and to loose its seven seals." (Revelation 5:5, NKJ)

John immediately stopped weeping and turned around to look at this magnificent King of kings, the victorious Lion of Judah, our Saviour and God. This is what he saw:

> "And I looked, and behold, in the midst of the throne and of the four living creatures, and in the midst of the elders, stood a Lamb as though it had been slain…"
>
> (Revelation 5:6, NKJ)

John was in the presence of God Almighty. He looked around the throne room, expecting to see a Lion, the only One in heaven and earth and under the earth who was worthy to open the seals. He did not find a lion or a strong, courageous Son of the Almighty God, a royal Prince. He found a slain lamb.

I had to get rid of the image of Jesus I was seeking. Like John, I was also looking for the brave King who could snap a finger, whose spit could heal blind eyes, whose command healed leprous skin and could resurrect the dead.

I wanted to find the Son of God with my mind. I had to search for the Son of Man with my heart.

The nurse acted on her own opinion when she told Resje that she had to walk before she would be discharged from hospital. The specialist was shocked to hear that Resje got off the bed and walked a few steps. After those initial steps in the hospital it took Resje weeks before she could walk again. Pain prevented her from moving. She was eventually discharged from the hospital, depending on me to carry her wherever she needed to go. She was seven years old and weighed 25 kilograms. I needed to change her dressings on her back and legs twice a day, witnessing the raw wounds and her naked fear. I saw her agony of trying to walk or to sit - excruciating suffering that is beyond words to describe. I heard the inconceivableness in her voice, the tears and screams. We watched the sport and games other children played, the normality of life most other people led. I sat with her and we watched how life passed us by.

During this time, I realized I was looking at life through physical eyes. Like John, I was looking for the Lion of Judah, at what I thought life was. However, Jesus appeared in the Heavenlies as a slain Lamb. When I eventually closed my physical eyes, my heart opened. When my broken, shattered heart opened, I saw somebody sitting with me. He knew as much about suffering as we did.

I sat there on top of the hill of Golgotha under my cross, watching this Man on His cross, until He gave His last breath. I simply sat there and looked Him in the eye. He was a bloody, beaten, humiliated, crushed and broken Man. I watched the betrayal of His friends and the mocking of the soldiers. I heard the silence of His heart. I witnessed the humiliation of Him being flogged. I experienced how the soldiers nailed Him to the cross and heard the insults of the people. I sat there for days and weeks, for months and years. I sat until His blood and tears fell on me. Finally, I heard His voice when He cried out in a loud voice to His Father:

> "Eli, Eli, lama sabachthani? that is, "My God, My God, why have You forsaken Me?"
>
> (Matthew 27:46, NKJ)

I found the slain Lamb, forsaken by God. I met the Son of Man.

And my heart opened up. At first, it was a tiny crack, then a bit wider until I embraced the Man of Sorrows. Isaiah described the Man I found:

> "He has no form or comeliness; and when we see Him, there is no beauty that we should desire Him. He is despised and rejected by men, a Man of sorrows and acquainted with grief. And we hid, as it were, our faces from Him; He was despised, and we did not esteem Him. Surely He has borne our griefs and carried our sorrows; yet we esteemed Him stricken, smitten by God, and afflicted." (Isaiah 53:2-4)

I sat until I understood, not everything, but a little, for now maybe enough.

He revealed His heart to me. Although He was a broken crushed Lamb, He had the heart of a Lion. He was brave, pure and holy. Looking at Him with physical eyes, like John, you can only see the slain Lamb. However, through the eyes of the heart, the slain Lamb becomes the Lion of Judah.

All He asked of me in return was to give Him my heart.

In Psalm 51:16-17 we read:

> "For You do not desire sacrifice, or else I would give it; You do not delight in burnt offering. The sacrifices of God are a broken spirit, a broken and a contrite heart – These, O God, You will not despise." (NKJ)

He wanted my broken heart. He gave me the reason why He wanted it in Isaiah:

> "... I dwell in the high and holy place, with him who has a contrite and humble spirit, to revive the spirit of the humble, and to revive the heart of the contrite ones." (Isaiah 57:15, NKJ)

He wanted me to give Him my heart so that He could heal it. It is easy to discard the emotions of anger, rejection and bitterness. It takes Almighty God to piece together a shattered heart, precisely what the plastic surgeon performed on Resje's back.

We are instructed in the Bible to change and to become like Jesus. Jesus did not only perform mighty deeds. He also suffered; was nailed to a wooden cross and died. I always thought to be like Jesus meant that we were holy and without sin, powerful in our walk with God and man. That is only one side of the coin. Golgotha and suffering lies on the other side.

Paul was God's chosen instrument to carry God's name before the Gentiles and the people of Israel. That involved a huge amount of suffering. It was the same with Resje. God chose her to become an instrument for Him to use. That instrument was an instrument of suffering. If we look at all this with the eyes of our flesh, we only see meaningless suffering and we are upset with God because He does not intervene.

However, if we look with our spiritual eyes, we see that she is slowly being changed into the image of Christ. Her suffering has a huge impact on many people. Many people have been touched by Resje's suffering, and many will still be.

To gaze upon her suffering is like looking upon the suffering of Jesus. Jesus asked God how could He forsake him, so did I.

Jesus felt lonely and beaten, so did I. Jesus was hurt, so was I. God looked upon Jesus' suffering and did nothing to prevent it. He did not send His Legions of Angels to rescue Him, in fact He sent Jesus to earth to be crucified. God looked upon us and turned His face away.

He chose Resje to be born with giant pigmented naevi. For her, He chose a road of pain and hurt, rejection and agony, suffering and tears.

Like Jesus and Paul, my blemished girl became God's chosen one.

Chapter Five

THE LAND OF MORIAH

In Genesis 22:2 God instructed Abraham:

> "Take now your son, your only son Isaac, whom you love, and go to the land of Moriah, and offer him there as a burnt offering on one of the mountains of which I shall tell you." (NKJ)

From the moment Resje was born, to the time I realized that she was a chosen instrument in God's hands, I regarded her as the one who would one day lead me to God. Day and night my prayers to God were filled with Resje and her healing. It is not that I did not care about anything else or that it did not matter to me. My soul overflowed with thoughts of Resje and her suffering; there simply was no place for anything else. Wherever I went and whatever I did, it centered on Resje, her suffering and her healing.

I began to feel very privileged. We were not only God's children, but He also chose us to walk the road of suffering. No ordinary person could handle so much suffering. I knew God gave Resje extraordinary power and strength to cope. I knew it was not us but His Holy Spirit who gave the strength to carry on. I was convinced that He had such a wonderful future and a destiny for Resje. Slowly, an element of elevation crept in. Because of Resje's suffering, I was humble enough not to have any outward manifestation of elevation or haughtiness, but deep in my heart – ah, yes, my heart again - there was definitely a feeling of we, above other people, were important and special in God's eyes. I thought maybe she would not only lead me out of Egypt, but many other people as well. Gradually, although later I could see the signs were there from the very beginning, she replaced Jesus. To me, she became something of a saviour, a messiah child.

At this stage, we were living on a farm in the North-West of Zimbabwe, sixty kilometers from the nearest small rural town of Chinhoyi.

God had to intervene in my life once again. He sent a young man and his wife from the southern tip of Africa, Cape Town, to two thousand kilometers north, to pastor our church in this little town. This young pastor had just completed seven years of formal theological studies at university. He was bright and had an intellectual view on spiritual matters. I immediately connected with him. He also held a secret in his heart. Unlike my dark secrets, his secret was a passionate heart for God like David. He did not only serve God with his mind, his heart was burning for the Kingdom of God.

God chose him and his wife, sending them deep into Africa to bring change to the lives of many people, including mine. We prayed and cried together until God revealed to him my heart. Although we were close friends by now, he was obedient to God. He came to see me on the farm. I sat opposite him eager to hear what God had revealed to him.

It was a short visit. He quickly finished his coffee, looked me straight in the eye and simply said the following: "Resje and her healing has become your god. This is an idol in the eyes of the Lord. You will need to sacrifice her as Abraham sacrificed his son, Isaac".

I was shattered. In three sentences, he had demolished everything that I had worked on in my walk with the Lord over the previous eight years. I felt special in God's eyes and now He reprimanded me. My cheeks burnt with shame. However, even more important than all my personal indignities and hurt, God asked of me the most precious thing in the world: my little girl. He was the one who gave me this girl to take care of, now He wanted me to give her up.

I came tumbling down. I thought I had reached the top of the mountain but I came sliding down faster than the climb. Fortunately, this time I did not hit rock bottom. My relationship with Jesus was stronger than before - a Rock stopped my fall.

My primary purpose was to discover the truth. Although I trusted my friend, my initial reaction was denial. I was convinced that God would never ask this of me. Through thorough self-examination, reality shockingly dawned on me: outside of Resje and my desire for her healing, there was nothing to say to, or ask, of God. I had become obsessed with her healing. What I had to do became clear the moment I recognized this - I had to crucify my desire for her healing.

The secondary purpose was to journey to a spiritual place called the Land of Moriah, alone with Resje to give her up. The thought of sacrificing her was of such magnitude to me, that I pushed it away. I had to go through my own Gethsemane and Golgotha before entering the Land of Moriah.

Our house on the farm was built on the lower slopes of a hill. I could not stay down in the valley. My Gethsemane was at the top. The top was a vigorous forty-minute climb. There was an old stone altar at the top, built by the locals in honour of their ancestors. It was built for demonic feasts where ancestral worship took place. I thought that was suitable for me. Daily, for three months I climbed the hill to reach the top to deal with the demons within me.

The first thing that I did was to demolish the demonic altar. I carried the heavy rocks as far as I could and threw them down the hill. Then I built my own altar, stacking seven huge rocks on top of one another. I anointed it with olive oil and sat down.

One more demon had to be fought before I could digest the words of my friend: I felt punished by God. Gone was the anger and rejection. Now, I was being flogged by God. He was punishing me for my sins and transgressions and for putting Resje first in my life. He was punishing me by not healing Resje. As the devil wanted it, I turned to the Old Testament and read how God punished His people. Book after book, generation after generation, He punished them. He became a cruel God with a whip in His hands, beating the life out of me. The more punished I felt, the more bitter I wanted to become. Because I had sat in the presence of Jesus for such a long time, I realized that all these emotions only harmed my perspective of God. When God told Job about all the animals He had created and how He cared for them, Job then confessed that up to then he had only heard of God, but after he had heard how God loves and cares for His creation, he now had seen God. That was my main aim all along. I wanted to see God and wanted to find out from Him why He did not want to become involved. If God told Job that He cared for animals, surely God cared more for people.

I had to apply faith in a loving God. I found that very difficult. Everywhere around me were the signs of an unloving and uncaring God. If He loved us, He would heal us. If He loved us, He would send rain. If He loved us, our loved ones would not die, or be born blind, or deaf or lose limbs or fight wars. Nevertheless, God says that we cannot understand Him and His ways and that we do not see the world as He does. I had to force myself to shut my physical ears and eyes to this world, only then another world and time emerged: eternity in heaven.

Father God was so concerned to see the people he created and loved going to hell, He sent His only son to walk a road of suffering temporarily, for mankind to be saved. In faith, I had to accept that the reason God did not answer my prayers, was that He loved me so much that His concern was where I would spend eternity. Resje brought me into contact with God. However, I had placed her between God and me, which prevented me from walking into the fullness of God. God's love goes deeper than ours. Humans understood that Resje filled my world; God wanted me to enter heaven, so that He could fill my world. Humans cared for my changing emotions; God cared for my eternal soul.

I looked into my own heart. I would rather have God heal Resje than God love me eternally. His love brought me no joy. It brought me tears and a heaviness in my soul. Resje and her healing meant more to me than God, who was only interested in my future and not in the present situation.

It moved me that Jesus suffered so much for me, but God's love did not really move me. It was a cold fact. It was as if God loved me for His sake. He wanted many souls one day in heaven to worship and praise Him for His sake. My present situation with all my dreams and desires did not matter to Him.

At first I simply sat next to my homemade altar, on top of the hill, overlooking a huge lake. I had nothing to ask of God. I knew what I had to do. I had to die to my dreams and hopes of seeing Resje healed. Then the sobs came. Out of my belly of hope, I had to bring a healed Resje forth and give her up. I had to gather up the dreams and desires for a perfect skin out of my innermost soul and stack it on the cold stones of the altar. I had to dig out the belief that she was chosen and place it on the altar.

My mind and thoughts were next. I learned from the vultures on the farm, observing how they picked at bits of flesh in carcasses. I picked at my thoughts of healing and restoration, of a future and a hope, of destiny and purpose. In strings and cords, they came out until a bare skeleton remained.

The last thing I had to do was to remove the very last bit of flesh: my heart. I took my heart out and put it on the altar. In the one room was fear and anger. I knew that it was good that that side of my heart was on the altar. However, in the other room of my heart was my life. It was pumping. The blood was filled with hope, desires, dreams and love – all for one little girl, my precious baby daughter. It was everything that I lived for. Like Jesus, in His Gethsemane, who told his disciples that His soul was "exceedingly sorrowful, even to death" (Matthew 26:38, NKJ), I had to die to everything I believed in. I had to strangle the life out of my heart. With my own hands, slowly and very painfully I pressed all the blood and life out of my heart.

Three months later, I knew I was empty of myself and knew that I had reached Golgotha.

How I wished that the Bible were more descriptive of the emotions of its characters. In Genesis 22:2, God asked of Abraham the most difficult thing in his life, to sacrifice his son, Isaac. Verse 3 simply says:

> "So Abraham rose early in the morning and saddled his donkey, and took two of his young men with him…" (NKJ)

I wonder how he spent that night. Did he sleep? Could he eat? What went on in his mind? Was he superhuman and slept peacefully throughout the night? I can understand the few written emotions of the superhuman Jesus because He was the Son of God. But Abraham? He was as human as I.

In Genesis 12, we read of one of Abraham's emotions. He was afraid for his own life. He was so scared to die that he pretended his wife, Sarah, was his sister, not caring that she was taken to the Pharaoh's house. The Pharaoh could do anything to Sarah, even sleep with her, as long as the people in Egypt did not kill him. Then ten chapters later, when he had to kill his own son, we simply read: "So, he rose early".

Could this be a characteristic of men in Biblical times? They did not know how to show their emotions when it came to their children. I read about Hannah. Hannah could not conceive. She begged God to give her a child. When God gave her a child, she returned the child to the priest, Eli, after he was weaned, far away from her home, so that Samuel could be brought up in the house of the Lord. Little Samuel must have been three or four, maybe five years old.

1 Samuel 1:27-28 (NKJ) simply says:

> "For this child I prayed, and the Lord has granted me my petition which I asked of Him. Therefore I also have lent him to the Lord; as long as he lives he shall be lent to the Lord…"

It was not only a characteristic of the men in Biblical times; women, too, simply gave up their children to God.

The realization gradually dawned that obedience to God was the key. My relationship with God had to go through another dimension to reach the point of obedience. Obedience was a sacrifice in itself. Obedience has nothing to do with emotions. You can cry, your soul can become exceedingly sorrowful or you can even fear death. However, there comes a time where you have to put all your emotions aside. You have to be obedient and take the cup the Father holds out to you. You have to be obedient to His voice when He commands you to drink from it, one sip at a time.

I knew I could stay in my Gethsemane and cry for the rest of my life. I know of many people who do. Nobody blames them for being there. Life is horrible to some, cruel to others. In general, life is not kind. If I had to end this book here, people would come up to me and cry and sympathize with me. We were given a raw deal, as many other people in this world. This is a sad place full of suffering.

I wonder if Jesus would have stayed in the Garden of Gethsemane forever, if God had not sent Judas and his gang to end His Son's pleas... with a kiss! I can imagine what would have happened. Jesus would have gathered all his disciples, explaining to them His sorrowful soul, telling them that God is not answering. The disciples would have quickly arranged for prayer meetings at different spots in the Garden, gathering more believers, initiating a prayer vigil. Thousands of believers would have gathered, praying, begging and pleading with God. This would have resulted in different reactions. Some would have become so furious with God they would have chosen to turn their backs on Him. Some would have blamed God. God can send deliverance and angels, but He is a harsh God, not wanting to help His own Son. Some people will simply give up, saying there is no purpose. A few will persevere, fast, pray and beg, trying to understand a God who cannot be understood.

If we remain in our own little gardens, we choose to stay angry or hurt, unforgiving or sad. We will never understand God. We will never eliminate suffering from this world. I always thought the kiss that Judas, the betrayer, gave Jesus was ironical. Now, I realize that this very kiss brought on the end of Jesus' suffering. It was time for Jesus to arise, to show His obedience to His Father.

My story was no different to that of Abraham. It was fairly simple. God called me to go to the Land of Moriah. Nothing was going to change His mind: no emotions, no debating, no prayer meetings with fasting and weeping. I had been to Gethsemane and reached Golgotha. Moriah was waiting. Like Abraham, I had to arise. Like Hannah, I had to return to Eli. Like Jesus, it was time to show my obedience to God.

I think Abraham and Hannah loved God more than they loved their children. I know Jesus loved God more than anything else. It was different for me, but there was one thing in my heart for God - trust. I trusted that He knew best. Because He told me that I had to sacrifice Resje, I knew I had to. I had to arise.

In Genesis 22:3 (NKJ), we read what Abraham did:

> "So Abraham rose early in the morning and saddled his donkey, and took two of his young men with him, and Isaac his son; and he split the wood for the burnt offering, and arose and went to the place of which God had told him."

I went up the hill one morning, taking our dogs with me for companions and protection. There were many deadly snakes on the farm, especially on the hill. There was one Snake whose purpose was to prevent me from reaching my final destination. The Land of Moriah was my final destination. I could not think of life beyond that.

I took Resje's hair curls from her very first haircut that I kept in my Bible with me. I kept it in a little envelope at a page that was very special to me. One day, after Resje's forty-eighth operation, I came across Isaiah 51:22 (NKJ):

> "Thus says your Lord, the Lord and your God, who pleads the cause of His people: 'See, I have taken out of your hand the cup of trembling, the dregs of the cup of My fury; you shall no longer drink it.'"

This portion of scripture stood out that day. It was God's Rhema Word to me. I understood it literally, interpreting that it indicated Resje's last operation. I believed God was taking this cup away from us. How I laughed and danced with joy when I read that. The envelope had found a new home. Whenever I felt we were not progressing, I would take her hair out and meditate on this scripture. When the operations continued, I reasoned that I had misunderstood the number of the operations, but that the end was in sight. God WILL take away the cup from us. He told me that Himself. Her healing is imminent. I needed patience because God's timing is not ours. He WILL heal her.

This was the scripture of hope that kept me going. Resje's hair was the most precious possession that I had of her, her crown of glory. It was the only part of her body that had no naevi. She had naevi on her head, but her hair was perfect. It was healthy, normal and beautiful. It embodied the promise of a healthy little girl.

I reached the top of the hill. No snake/Snake hindered me. The wind was a soft breeze. I opened the envelope, taking everything out, not wanting to keep anything. I threw the curls into the wind, looked up and shouted at the top of my voice: "I will sacrifice her! I will sacrifice her!! I will sacrifice her!!!"

The wind took her hair. I saw the curls disappearing in the wind. But the wind came back. It dried the tears on my cheeks.

Hours later, I climbed down with more questions in my heart than ever before.

What do You want me to do now, God? How do You want me to sacrifice her? Surely, You do not want me to pick up a knife and sacrifice her the way You asked of Abraham. Do You want me not to take care of her anymore? Do You want me to stop taking her to hospitals? Do You want us to stop the operations? Do You want me to stop rubbing her back? Do You want me to stop going to her in the night? How do You want me to sacrifice her?

I could not sleep, not thinking of anything else. God had to show me how He wanted me to sacrifice Resje, I had no idea. What was on His mind? My pastor-friend and his wife started praying with me.

One day I was returning from lecturing at the University of Zimbabwe in Harare. It was a two-hour trip to the farm, a journey I undertook twice a week. I had a full week's lecture load that the University allowed me to condense into two days.

Traveling long distances in Zimbabwe is normal. The four hours traveling meant I could devote myself fully to speaking to God. As I left Harare on that particular day, I prayed once again that I did not know how the sacrifice was to take place. I was willing to do whatever He wanted me to do. The next moment God spoke to me. He spoke to me as clearly as if He was sitting next to me in the car. I was fully conscious and of sound mind, I was not in a trance-like state or anything like that. There were no outward manifestations that I was in the presence of God. I did not shake or tremble. I was driving my car and continued to drive. He spoke silently to me in my thoughts, yet I clearly heard His voice. It was soft and gentle, yet filled with authority.

He instructed me to write and perform a one-woman play called, *"The secrets of Mary."* He told me to use the example of a modern woman who believed that her son, Jesus, was given to her to become King. Contrary to her belief, He did not become King but died on a cross. God wanted me to adapt a contemporary view of how people digest something that happens in contrast to what they believe in. In the Biblical account, Mary, mother of Jesus, never expressed her anger or fear. Modern women do. They become angry and fight, they cry and scream, they turn to alcohol and away from God. The play was to be written in two acts. The first was to portray Mary's anger towards God when her son dies and does not become the King as she was told. In the second act, Mary discovers that she misunderstood God. He did not mean an earthly king, but a heavenly King. This act had to portray her joy in discovery of the true meaning. His last words were the most important to me. In the process of writing and performing the play, it would become clear to me how to sacrifice Resje.

I started writing immediately. I sat in front of the computer and the words and thoughts just came. Within three months, I had written and rehearsed the play. During the next two years, I was invited by different churches to perform the play at various venues in Zimbabwe and South Africa. In one scene, Mary gives a long loud scream when the soldiers hammer the first nail into the hand of Jesus. The scream symbolized the death of her dreams. Whenever I came to that particular scene, it was not only the character Mary who performed it. It was an opportunity for me to show the whole world the rawness of my pain. I did not need words to express my feelings. One raw, loud scream out of my belly ended my dreams and hopes that I had for Resje.

The play was a huge success. Before performances, I shared with the audience a little of Resje's background and how I identified with the character, Mary. People would sit glued to their chairs for two hours, rushing forward after the performance. They could also identify with this modern Mary. They openly shared with me their pain and hurt, anger and secrets. I cried and prayed with them, meeting many people who walked with hidden hurt in their hearts.

Nearly a year after my first performance I realized what was happening to me. I still loved Resje more than anything else. I continued caring for her, rubbing her back, getting up at night, taking her to hospital, but my thoughts and prayers were now filled with the broken people I met. It slowly dawned on me. I'd done it! I'd sacrificed her! God did not want me to take up a knife to kill my own child. God wanted me to sacrifice her in my mind and thoughts. He wanted me to notice the suffering of other people. Resje still had the number one place in my heart, but she had shrunk and my heart had more room for others.

From that moment on there was a purpose in my scream. A new hope replaced the futility of it.

Those two years performing "The secrets of Mary," brought me much happiness. Portraying Mary's pain was really my pain. From the moment Resje was born, I had wanted to share her suffering with the rest of the world, but nobody really had the time or energy to listen. Everyone though, had the time for an evening out to attend a performance. For two hours, I had the stage to myself to show the world our pain. In addition to this, God knew of my secret desires to be an actress, from when I was a young girl. I used to stand in front of the mirror in my room, practising how to weep and laugh. I loved drama. I had won gold medals in eisteddfods, taken drama lessons, received an honorary school blazer for outstanding performance in drama and studied drama at university. Acting was an unfulfilled dream and desire.

God knew this. When I was obedient to Him and willing to give up Resje for Him, He granted me some of my heart's deepest and hidden desires: He let me act for Him. I will always be thankful to God for letting me be creative for Him, hopefully touching many lives through performing "The secrets of Mary".

At the age of 40, God kept speaking to me through His Word that He was going to bless us with a little boy. Five years later, when I thought I was much too old for babies a healthy, beautiful baby boy, Emil, was born with perfect skin. At that stage Resje was 12 years old.

Now, we had a new baby in our lives. We were doing well financially. I thought this was the season of God's blessings. The excitement of the prosperity bandwagon became tempting. There are enough examples in the Bible of how God blessed His people financially by increasing their possessions. I was beginning to relax spiritually.

I kept a diary of Resje's operations with photographs of each operation. A medical record of her progress would be a good thing to have. After each operation I recorded the number of stitches, where the surgeon had operated, what he had done, how she recovered, some personal details, and so on. The diary and photo-album became very precious to me.

And then, in 2000, the President of Zimbabwe, Robert Mugabe and his government, adopted a violent land resettlement program. For the next two years we had numerous threatening experiences on our farm. War veterans were sent onto the farms of commercial farmers to invade and harass. They threatened to take over the farm and kill us. At first, we did not take the threats seriously, but after two years and many serious and unbelievable reports of what happened on other farms, their threats became real.

With a new, healthy baby in my arms, I could not imagine that our lives would change drastically once again.

On 9 August 2001, about seventy war veterans invaded our farm and lives. They managed to surround us, preventing us from leaving the house. They were drinking, armed with spears and axes, their eyes filled with hatred and murder. As the day progressed, they became more intoxicated, wild and violent. The police were alerted early in the morning, but were instructed by higher authorities not to react or interfere. The four of us were alone.

Watching their aggressiveness and drunken behaviour, I became convinced that it was the day we were to die. I concluded that we had reached the climax of our lives and God had decided to end it. After a long and intensive walk with God, many things in our lives were still wrong: curses that never turned into blessings; hidden and unknown sins; I did not do the many things that I wanted to do for Him; I could not sort out my life and the lives of my family here on earth. All the striving and the reasoning brought me nowhere. I was a sinner and fell short of the glory of God. All the individual thoughts became a dark symphony with death as the crescendo.

Miraculously, after ten traumatic hours, the four of us managed to escape, fleeing for our lives. This time I knew for sure we had God on our side. Despite the curses, the sins, our unholy lives, He had heard our prayers and saved our lives. He had fought for us. That night the drunken hordes forced their way into our house and destroyed everything that we owned, including Resje's valuable medical records.

However, the enemy could not destroy our lives, souls and spirits. And the enemy could not destroy the memories we will always carry with us of life on a farm in Zimbabwe.

The UNDP (United Nations Development Programme) requested a report of what happened that day on the farm. I could not sit down to write a cold 10-point report of what had happened. I wrote the following article (which is also available on the internet) of how our lives were invaded:

FLEEING FOR OUR LIVES: TWO TREE HILL FARM, ZIMBABWE – 2001

My husband, Charl Geldenhuys – a true Zimbabwean in all aspects of life, worked as a farm manager for Mr. Les de Jager on Two Tree Hill Farm, in the district of Makonde in Chinhoyi, Zimbabwe, for nearly five years, before I met him in South Africa. After our marriage we lived and worked for a couple of years in South Africa. Charl wanted me to see Two Tree Hill Farm one holiday, and I immediately fell in love with it. In 1992, Charl got his old job back with Les, we moved to Two Tree and I, a city-girl, became a farmer's wife.

This farm was paradise. Apart from growing crops, like maize, Soya beans, winter wheat, tobacco and Hypericum flowers, there was also a lot of game on the farm. We had six hand reared baby elephant, we bottle fed six giraffe, eland and zebra were relocated from drought areas, we also had herds of kudu, tsessebe, sable, reedbuck and impala. In addition we had over 260 recorded species of birds. The farm has a huge beautiful dam, renowned for its bass and bream, yielding two all Africa records. Instead of shopping in beautiful arcades, seeing the latest movie, going to the theater, my highlights became completely different. I now was riding the tame elephant, going out onto the dam with a boat or with the canoe, fishing for bass or bream, putting live earthworms on as bait (myself!) and watching game on horseback. To still be in touch with the other side of life, I accepted a lectureship at the University of Zimbabwe in the Department of Modern Languages.

Charl did not allow anyone to shoot on the farm, not even birds. All life was regarded as very precious. We had a very tame eland, which we named Em. Em was in love with my husband, and I think Charl was a little bit in love with her too. Every time he passed Em, whether it was on his motorbike or with the pick-up, he had to stop to greet her. She would put her head on his shoulders and he had to rub her forehead. Whenever I was with Charl, she would push me aside, looking me straight in the eye, as if she wanted to say this was her special boyfriend and this was her time with him now.

Early in 2000 we sat down together one Sunday night at 8 o'clock, to watch the ZBC news. We both could not believe our eyes and ears as we witnessed the first farm invasion by war veterans in the district of Beatrice, south of Harare.

Coming from South Africa, I had always commented on the good racial relationships people in Zimbabwe had. I told all my ex-colleagues from universities in South Africa that the students and lecturers at the University of Zimbabwe were the best I had ever had. Watching this news, I realized this would have far reaching results. All of a sudden, overnight, our carefree, peaceful existence on a farm in Africa was something of the past.

On the 26th March 2000 we had our first encounter with the war veterans, invading our farm and lives. About a hundred of them surrounded the house early one morning, barricading us into the house. They wanted Charl. My daughter, Resje, then 11 years old, could not get to school. She had to watch the gates and the fence, to observe if they should get violent. I was pregnant at that stage with our second child, a very late pregnancy for me, but planned. All three of us were over the moon with the pregnancy. I kept telling myself to remain calm, prayed and waited anxiously for the police to resolve this invasion.

When the police arrived in the afternoon, they produced a search warrant. Somebody alleged that we had an armory in the house and nine officials (some from Chinhoyi police station, some from the President's Office and some CIO) searched our house. Room after room they searched. Charl and I had to stand in front of them while they searched. They opened all our cupboards and drawers, looked behind paintings and underneath carpets for hidden cellars. They opened ever bag, every suitcase, and every closed container in the house. They went through my daughter's underclothes, then through mine. They pushed my sanitary towels away to see what was under them. They checked every firearm's license, then counted the ammunition one by one. Having had nothing to do with police before in my life, I found this invasion of our privacy very humiliating. Charl was ashen. He couldn't get a word out. Then I suddenly thought of the possibility that somebody could have framed us and maybe hidden some firearms in the house or somewhere in the outside buildings. I could sense that was Charl's concern too. I was trying to think how would we ever be able to convince everybody that we were innocent. In the light of the present political situation, I knew this would be a triumph for them. But God was good to us. They found nothing. They had to leave the farm without arresting us. Only then could we turn to Resje. She kept thinking they were going to march us out of the farm and out of her life, and was trying to make plans where she could hide and how she could let somebody know that she was still alive and still in the house.

The second invasion took place a few months later, on a Saturday. Once again, in Resje's presence. She had to watch the gates while we were trying to get help on the farmer's internal radio network. Once again the police came out later in the day and eventually resolved the matter.

It was my school lift-run duty by the third invasion. Charl was alone on the farm. Each time the war vets became more and more aggressive. By now they realized they had more and more power and the farmers could not do anything. There was a complete breakdown of law and order and we could not trust the police anymore. This time they tried to axe my husband, but he managed to outwit them.

On the 6th August 2001 a farmer in our community asked for assistance from his neighbors as war vets were trying to enter his house. His

110

neighbors responded. Charl was attending a security meeting and could not go. When they arrived, the war vets stoned and beat them. The farmers, after months of restraint, reacted. By the time the police arrived, the war vets were gone. The police asked the farmers to go to the police station in Chinhoyi to file their reports. Once they were inside the police station they were arrested. Others who went to the police station later that afternoon to find out what had happened were arrested too. A total of 21 white men were arrested. After they had spent 16 days in jail an unrealistically high bail was granted to them, but they were not allowed to return to their farms or the province for four weeks.

On Tuesday, the 7th August, black men beat up dozens of white women and elderly white men in Chinhoyi. It was as if a racial war had started in Chinhoyi town. Each time they asked the same question: "Are you a farmer's wife?" Without waiting for an answer, they tripped and beat up the women. White people were warned on the Community Radio Network not to come to or proceed through Chinhoyi.

On Thursday morning, the 9th August at 5.50 a.m., one of Charl's drivers came roaring into the workshop on a tractor, shouting loudly. I immediately knew this was something more serious than before. I shouted at Resje to put on her running shoes. I immediately got dressed and put on some running shoes too. I thought if we had to run for our lives today, at least we should have some good shoes on. The baby, Charl-Emil, started crying and for the rest of the day I could not put him down for a moment. He instinctively knew something was not right, and he refused to sleep. About 10 war vets shouted at Charl to come out. He went out to the gate, which was locked, and I heard them shouting: "We want you out. We want you out here! We want to see your blood flow! Come out! Come out here!" I started praying because I knew that it was only God who could save us now.

Charl tried to pacify them with no success and came back into the house. We locked all the doors and then Resje had (once again) the task to watch three gates and the fence. Charl immediately contacted our security firm and the police. It was 6 a.m. The war vets had chopped a jacaranda tree down across the only access road so as to prevent us from leaving the farm in our cars. We called for help on the radio, but because of what *happened the Monday with the 21 men, we were afraid that this was yet another planned trap to get more white men arrested. A couple of farmers arrived, but they remained at the tar road, 10 kilometers from the house. I started phoning our pastor, friends and family to pray for us. I realized that this was some evil force controlling the people, and that God alone could save us.*

The war vets started looting our workshop and shed, which were 100 meters from our house. For nine hours I watched young and old men and women and their children (as young as 10 years old), carrying 50 kg. bags of fertilizer on their shoulders, loading it onto our trailers and carting it off with our nine tractors and trailers. They stayed away about 25 minutes, offloading it somewhere and then returned with more and more people. Coming back to loot some more, they were getting drunker, shouting triumphantly, becoming more aggressive and wild.

We were due to leave for our annual holiday on Saturday, the 11th August. Charl then told me to start packing for the holiday. He thought if we did get a chance to get off the farm, we should go on our holiday two days earlier. I did that under much pressure. Resje saw one man with mad eyes trying to climb the fence. She was convinced he was going to kill her father and mother. Then, she thought, she would be alone in the house with the baby. Every now and then she started sobbing and screaming uncontrollably. I then had to go and shake her to try and calm her. Charl-Emil was getting heavier and heavier. My back wanted to break. My responsibilities were communications - the radio and telephone. Charl was in a desperate state. He kept running through the house with a gun in each hand, studying their movements. Twelve-year-old Resje could not move. Charl relied on her to keep him informed what the war vets were doing at the gates and potential areas of penetration in the security fence.

Whenever we go on holiday our Cook cares for the dogs. I was concerned about how we could leave without the Cook's having the keys to access the fridge for dog food. We had 2 big Boerboel dogs, 3 Australian Cattle Dogs and 8 puppies. It was impossible to put them in the car too. I then suggested to Charl to go out and shoot all the dogs. He kept saying he could not do that in Resje's presence. Resje had been hysterical so many times by then that I thought she would have to get over this one too.

Eventually Charl shouted at me asking me what I thought the war vets would do if he started firing shots. That brought some reality to me. But then I thought maybe it would be better for our dogs if we slit their throats than leave them at the mercy of rampaging looters. Charl was horrified by this suggestion. Then I thought, I would have to do it. I'd get a knife and go out and slit the throats of all 13 dogs. I waited for the opportune moment.

At 11 o'clock one guy came right up to the gate and shot at one of our dogs with a catapult. I saw that and wondered what was going on.

In the meantime, we kept phoning the police to find out where they were. We told them things were getting out of hand and we needed help urgently. They kept saying they were on their way. The police station is about 50 kilometers from the farm – 25 minutes traveling time!

At 12 o'clock the same man with the catapult and another man came right up to the gate. This time he had an axe in his hand instead of the catapult. With one quick movement he axed the lock and the gate flung wide open. Our Boerboel dog, the one which had been shot at earlier, challenged the intruders. The man discarded the axe, drew out a pistol and gave her one shot. She fell dead instantly. Resje and I both screamed at the top of our voices that the gate was open and that they had killed our dog. Charl unlocked the back door and ran out to face about 70 war vets. He shouted at the top of his voice: "Get away from here! Get away! Get away from this gate! Get away!!" I ran to the door, and shouted at Charl to come back into the house immediately. As he turned to come back, the same man fired a shot at him, missing him. I thought 70 war vets were going to rush in and kill us all.

I called Resje and explained to her that the reason why we live is to die one day, and that day was today and in a short while we would all be together in heaven with God. Nothing and no one can take us away from God.

The gate remained wide open for the next three hours, the dog lying dead in her own blood, 70 war vets walking up and down right next to the gate. Yet, nobody even attempted to set a foot into the garden. I am convinced an angel of the Living God prevented them.

Charl took me aside and told me to start packing what was important to me, because he anticipated that they would start looting the house next.

Packing for the holiday already took my last bit of sanity. It was an impossible task to pack what was important to me. I opened Resje's cupboard. All of a sudden I could not choose a dress that was more important than the other. Everything in that cupboard was important to me and yet, nothing was important. The only important thing in this world, at that stage, was for all four of us to get off the farm alive. I left all the suitcases on the floor, empty. I could not do it. It was mad to think of packing some goods, while 70 war vets could storm the house to kill us at any moment. On top of that, I had a crying baby, a hysterical daughter, a shouting husband, a ringing telephone and a calling radio.

In any case how do you pack up your life of 46 years in a suitcase?

At 3 p.m., 9 hours later, the police arrived. Not alone. Minister Chombo, Mr Philip Chiyangwa, a Member of Parliament, and Governor Chanetsa accompanied them. With them were a couple of journalists with clicking cameras and ZBC with their video cameras. I was immensely relieved. I thought that at last ZBC could show the world what really happened here today. I ran out of the house with Charl and Charl-Emil on my hip. Charl asked Resje to stay behind to man the radio.

Minister Chombo took a seat on a heap of looted fertilizer bags and prepared himself to look good on camera. He told us to sit down, but there were only looted fertilizer bags and neither Charl nor I wanted to touch it. Mr. Chombo's first sentence highlighted the harsh reality of a sick Zimbabwe. He pointed at Charl and accused him of being responsible of what had happened here today. I could not believe my ears. His next accusation sent shivers down my spine: "So, you shot at this innocent man here, missed him, and killed your own dog today". I immediately recalled the man with the catapult at 11 o'clock, and realized all this was planned. This was an orchestrated, planned and rehearsed devilish scheme to scare us off the farm.

Charl and I were not given an opportunity to defend ourselves, or to talk. The journalists and interviewers were obviously told not to ask us any questions or to have any contact with us. We both stood there, shaking our heads. His next set of accusations shattered all my hopes for a politically stable country. He accused Charl of burning the war vets' houses and grass and of chasing their cattle into his own paddock. Charl was not given opportunity to deny these false allegations. He then told Charl that the government of Zimbabwe had placed the war vets on our farms, they were there legitimately, and if Charl had a problem with them, he should go to the government or to him personally, and not take it out on these law-abiding citizens. I thought I was going to wake up from a terrible nightmare. I kept thinking, "Charl is a Zimbabwean citizen. The government of a country and most definitely the police of a country are supposed to protect their citizens, not falsely accuse them. Why are they not helping Charl? Why are they against their own citizens? We love this country. Charl works so hard on this farm to produce food for the people. Why do they not appreciate him?"

They kept trying to aggravate Charl. I kept praying for Charl to remain calm. When minister Chombo eventually stood up to go, I had the feeling that they were very disappointed in our behavior. They wanted to create a scene, and had all the cameras there to film our response. They did not expect Charl to remain that calm. As they left, the minister turned around and said they would leave us two policemen to protect us from any harm. His final words were: "See, how good we are to you". Two minutes after they left, the policemen said they had to confiscate all Charl's weapons. It took them a very long time to collect all the weapons and check all the licenses. They left with all the weapons to return immediately, saying that the minister instructed them to remove all the ammunition too. With that they departed, leaving us all alone, disarmed, with hordes of criminals and war vets lurking in the surrounding bush. It was 4 o'clock.

I called on the farmers on the tar road to come and help us to remove the tree and get us off the farm. Two farmers were with us within 5 minutes, while a third was standing watch at the tar road.

I thought now was the time for me to re-think packing my important things in, however we realized that the war vets were regrouping for further aggression. We threw our holiday suitcases in the car, locked the door, and gave instructions to the foreman and the cook, who had miraculously appeared after our interview with the minister. It took us 15 minutes to pack and load.

I ran up the stairs leading to the garage and thought that in a million years I would never ever have thought that I would one day have to flee for my life.

We drove off the farm with our two vehicles, our holiday clothes for two weeks and a farm pick-up with a motorbike on.

We spent the night in Chinhoyi and left on Friday morning for South Africa. On Saturday we heard that they not only looted the house, but also trashed and completely destroyed it. Not a single piece of furniture was left in the house. The piano was chopped into pieces. All our books were put in the center of the one room and were burnt. They removed not only the windows but the frames as well. Doors were cut out of their frames with axes. They removed the roof completely. They demolished the toilets and basins.

Every cent that Charl and I ever earned went into the house, the books, clothes, paintings, shoes, CD's, sports equipment, furniture, bedding, curtains, kitchenware and everything else.

All of this was taken from us in one day, by a horde of criminals, supported by the police, and instigated by members of the government of Zimbabwe.

I keep wondering why I did not think of my Master's thesis, why not of all our photographs, our birth certificates, our wedding pictures, our degrees and diplomas, our Bibles, my jewellery, my diary, the record of our daughter's 66 operations with photo albums showing her progress. I remember then how I had walked through the house for nine hours, praying out loud: "Jesus, help us! Jesus, save our lives! God, have mercy on us! Jesus, stop them from stealing further! Oh God, please make them go away! Jesus, help us! Jesus, help us! Jesus, help us!"

I guess I was too occupied with our lives, than to think of the things that gave meaning to our lives.

Going back to Two Tree after our holiday showed me the destructive nature of evil. While I was walking from one empty room to another demolished room, this vast nothingness dawned on me – it is as if we no longer have a past.

Maybe that is how Em, our Eland, felt when they slaughtered her. Maybe she also felt that she never existed.

This time I did not slide off the mountain. I reached the top of my mountain, staring unbelievably at a second much higher mountain. I had thought that I only had to reach one mountaintop in a lifetime. Now, there in front of me, towered another mountain. I did not know if I had the strength for another climb. Yet, I knew without any doubt, God wanted me to get off this mountain and ascend the next one.

I did not have to start the climb from the bottom. There was an overall sense of immense joy that lifted me to halfway up the second mountain. Temporary feelings of anger and disappointment made me take a few dips to the bottom, but they were short-lived.

For the first time, I realized that my present life and not only everlasting life meant something to God. God ordered from the Heavenlies that the enemy was not to touch our lives. They could destroy all our material possessions, but my life and the lives of my family were sacred to God. Because God had saved our lives, He would take care of our material needs. Joy and peace flooded my soul. I meant something to God. My life was worth preserving. It was not only my life, He had also preserved the lives of the people most dear to me: my husband, Resje and our new baby.

After our three-week holiday in South Africa, we went back to Zimbabwe. We could not go back to the farm, so we stayed in a rented home in the little town of Chinhoyi. While we were on holiday in South Africa, a friend of ours mentioned his interest in immigrating to New Zealand. When I heard the name New Zealand, a chill went up my spine. The name also appealed to Charl. Although we knew no one in New Zealand, we applied for permanent residence, asking God to open doors if that was His will. Nine months later we were granted permanent residence. We stayed in Zimbabwe for a further seven months, hoping in vain for the situation to improve. When we left on December 21, 2002, God said to me: "Shake the Zimbabwean dust off your shoes." After a lengthy farewell to our friends and family in South Africa, we left South Africa, arriving in Christchurch at midnight on February 6, 2003, to begin a new life in a new country. I took the first step on New Zealand soil and heard God tenderly saying: "This is your new home."

A gush of life spread through me.

I thought I had arrived. Not many people have two mountains on their life path. Clearly, I had made it, or so I thought.

I have discovered that when you climb a high and dangerous mountain, people are all around you. A few may try to bring you down, but in general your friends who are there with you have one purpose only and that is to help you reach the top. They have your best interests at heart. They push you up, tie rope around you, secure you, climb a little with you and take hold of your hand when you slip. I had family and friends all around me on my journey. They prayed with me, stood by me, surrounded, encouraged and helped me make it to the top. I read somewhere that a true friend is someone who laughs, cries and prays with you. I made many true friends. My family not only supported us, they became my closest friends. Whenever my friends laughed with me, their laughter made the climb easier. The tears of friends falling onto the ground turned into rocks, big enough for me to secure my climb, preventing me from sliding. When the climb became too difficult, their prayers lifted me so that I could soar like an eagle.

I wonder if Job would have made it by himself. He had friends who surrounded him. Not all the advice given to him was good. In fact, very little of it was good. Their advice and ways of thinking were virtually all wrong, but they kept Job mentally alert and alive. He could think and meditate on what they said, arguing and reasoning with them. Their input was so important that they joined Job in the second chapter and remained with him for the rest of the book of Job. Forty chapters in the Bible are devoted to the important role of Job's friends.

At first, they sat with him. For seven days and seven nights, not one of them said a word. They sat with Job and grieved with him. Everyone who has experienced a lot of suffering will tell you how important that is. You need someone to sit with you, hold your hand and grieve with you. A true friend does not have to speak or provide answers for suffering. Who of us knows the mind of Christ to give answers anyway?

A true friend simply sits at your side.

That is exactly what my true friends did. They sat with me. Family and friends are like a bottle of good red wine. You have to open a bottle so that it can breathe. The same applies with friends. You need to be able to breathe in the presence of your friends, and so do they need to breathe in your presence. The longer a bottle of wine is opened, the more it breathes. Each friend has a specific aroma, which is their individual personality, their own distinct flavour. No friend tastes the same and I could learn something different from everyone. In New Zealand, I came to know the true meaning of room temperature. In the much warmer South Africa and Zimbabwe, one really needs to chill your red wines during the hot summer months. In the much cooler New Zealand, room temperature means it is not warmer or colder than the comfortable room temperature. True friends are the same temperature as your skin. They understand and compliment you, encourage you and build you up. They are a positive influence in your life, embracing you in the comfort of their warmth. The better the wine, the fuller the taste. Friends, who are healthy and strong, fully developed and secure, bring out the fullness in you. Wine comes from pressing grapes. A true friend is one who has undergone the treatment of pressing and squeezing. Life has molded them into wine. The wine develops a mature taste if it is allowed to grow old. Mature people have much life experience. The most distinctive characteristic of red wine is the colour red. This reminds me of blood. A blood covenant goes much deeper than your skin. When there is emotional bonding with a special friend it goes deeper than the skin.

Bread eaten without wine is dry and difficult to swallow, as a meal without friends. Without friends, laughter and fellowship, life is dry and lonely.

We started a new life in New Zealand, full of zeal and with much hope in our hearts. We did not know anybody. Slowly I realized that there was no longer wine at our meals. Our friends and family did not come with us. We were alone. Nobody knew how much Resje had suffered. I did not share the detailed account and extent of her suffering. Firstly, I did not want to dwell in the past - life was moving on. Secondly, people were busy and worked hard and did not have the time to sit with me. People were very friendly but they kept their distance and I kept mine. I made friends, friends who laughed, cried and prayed with me, but somehow I did not want them to come too close to me. I became quite lonely.

Another mountain stretched out in front of me. It had no dangerous cliffs or rocks. It was not a high mountain. A long, monotonous mountain stretched out "to infinity and beyond", in the words of Buzz Lightyear.

In the past high peaks had been quite a challenge to reach. This mountain was very different. There was no challenge. Life was not difficult in New Zealand, neither was it easy. There was no burning passion or fire in my heart. I survived, but was not bubbling with life. I was content, yet not filled with joy and happiness.

The monotony of everyday life crept into my soul. Cleaning, preparing meals and driving the children to school were slowly suffocating me. I did not want to walk around with death in my eyes but there was a lack of energy to start climbing this mountain. It was like a spiritual depression.

It was on this mountain that I realized I could not make it on my own. I needed someone to walk with me, someone who knew me, and what we had gone through, someone who knew my thoughts and my heart. My old friends did not know my new life. My new friends did not know my old life. I needed some God to walk with me. I needed the Holy Spirit. By now I knew doing things my way was not the best. Nevertheless, I found God's way difficult and could not make it on my own. I turned to the Beatitudes. It looked impossible to follow God. I could not be perfect the way God was perfect.

I trusted God and believed that He knew best, yet there was something missing in my walk with Him. Of the things missing were: joy, power, peace and authority.

We read in Luke 23:26-31 (NKJ) the following:

> "Now as they led Him away, they laid hold of a certain man, Simon a Cyrenian, who was coming from the country, and on him they laid the cross that he might bear it after Jesus.
>
> And a great multitude of the people followed Him, and women who also mourned and lamented Him.
>
> But Jesus, turning to them, said, 'Daughters of Jerusalem, do not weep for Me, but weep for yourselves and for your children.
>
> For indeed the days are coming in which they will say, "Blessed are the barren, wombs that never bore, and breasts which never nursed!"
>
> Then they will begin to say to the mountains, "Fall on us!" and to the hills, "Cover us!"
>
> For if they do these things in the green wood, what will be done in the dry?'"

Jesus received strength to preach the moment Simon picked up His cross. He warned them of even more difficult times to come. Jesus on His way to Golgotha, carrying His own cross, also could not make it on his own. He needed help, someone to carry His burden for Him.

I needed someone to carry my burden.

As always, I looked at Resje to learn from her. Like her first words when she learned to speak, asking her mommy to help, I turned to Father God with the same words: "Help…. help Father God…. help me, Father God!"

PART THREE

LIVING WATER IN DESERT CIRCLES

Chapter Six

THE FLOODPLAIN OF THE JORDAN

The prophet Elijah went to look for a successor and God directed him to Elisha. The two of them became best friends. They laughed, cried and prayed together. They were inseparable. Elisha followed Elijah everywhere and felt he could not live without him. When God decided it was time for Elijah to leave his temporary home, Elisha attached himself to Elijah and refused to leave him.

We read in 2 Kings how God forced Elisha to be on his own in his walk with Him. His friend, Elijah, guided him in this walk, but the time came for Elisha to build his own relationship with God. Elijah tried to persuade him at various places to leave him, but Elisha was reluctant. He kept following Elijah to different places. God had to intervene before Elisha could face the floodplain of the Jordan alone.

> "Then Elijah said to Elisha, 'Stay here, please, for the Lord has sent me on to Bethel.' But Elisha said. 'As the Lord lives, and as your soul lives, I will not leave you!' So they went down to Bethel." (2 Kings 2:2, NKJ)

> "Then Elijah said to him, 'Elisha, stay here, please, for the Lord has sent me on to Jericho.' But he said, 'As the Lord lives, and as your soul lives, I will not leave you!' So they came to Jericho." (2 Kings 2:4, NKJ)

> "Then Elijah said to him, 'Stay here, please, for the Lord has sent me on to the Jordan.' But he said, 'As the Lord lives, and as your soul lives, I will not leave you!' So the two of them went on."
>
> (2 Kings 2:6, NKJ)

The two of them came to the River Jordan. Elijah struck the water with his mantle, opening a dry passage across the river. They crossed over to the other side. Fifty other prophets of God remained, observing from a distance. On reaching the other side, God took Elijah away in a chariot of fire, leaving Elisha alone. As a memento or maybe something more than that, Elijah dropped his mantle. Elisha was on the opposite side of the Jordan that, by then, had returned to its normal flow, separating him from fifty other brothers.

It is interesting to note that God allowed Elisha to have Elijah as a watchful and prayerful companion at Bethel and Jericho, but when they reached Jordan, God decided that Elisha was ready to enter into a relationship with Him on his own.

Bethel was the place where Abram called on the name of the Lord, before his name was changed to Abraham. When Jacob met God in a dream and promised Jacob that He would be with him, Jacob called the place Bethel. When I reached the place where God held out His hand to me, I knew that I had reached the destination of my Bethel. I was not alone; I had the prayers of my parents to accompany me. They prayed, God responded to their prayers and chose me to walk with Him. Like Elisha in 2 Kings, I was not alone at Bethel.

Jericho was the city where the walls came tumbling down. I was surrounded by friends, pastors and family, when all my walls of resistance came tumbling down. They all cared for me, prayed with me, sustained me. Once again, like Elisha, I was not alone when I reached my Jericho.

When we moved to New Zealand, I realized that New Zealand is further away from Africa than any other country in the world. It was not only the River Jordan but also the vast ocean that distanced me from my physical and spiritual family. I faced the floodplain alone. The others were on the other side. It came at a crucial point in my life. It came when I realized I could not live in my own strength as God's follower. I needed help. The only memento or maybe something more than that was given to me by a dear friend. It was very similar to Elijah's mantle - a prayer shawl from Israel.

At a party, the host usually delights in introducing you to new people. I knew that I was filled with the Holy Spirit and that the strength I needed to live each day came from Him, but the Holy Spirit was as strange to me as strangers at a party. Just as I had sat at the feet of Jesus and had to learn to know Him, now I had to learn to know the Holy Spirit. I had no one to introduce me to Him. My spiritual family was on the other side of the world.

Once again I had to go to the beginning. When Jesus was still alive, He sent out His disciples in His strength so that they could perform many miracles. When Elijah ascended into heaven, he dropped his mantle for Elisha to pick up and use. Similarly when Jesus ascended into heaven, He promised that He would send us His Spirit so that we would not be alone.

I had to find Elijah's mantle quickly to be introduced to the Holy Spirit.

Because Peter, one of the disciples of Jesus, was an emotional man, I could identify with him. He pledged sincerely that he would follow Jesus to prison and death. He must have meant every word that he said, believing that his word was his honour. Jesus knew the hearts of men. He knew that we would fail Him, betray Him, forsake Him and deny Him. When Adam and Eve ate of the forbidden fruit in the Garden of Eden its juice comprised of deception and failure. Not one of us is good or holy or worthy to fulfill life's challenges. Within twenty-four hours of Peter pledging to follow Jesus unconditionally, he denied Him. Not once, but three times.

After rising from the dead, Jesus instructed the disciples to wait in Jerusalem until they had received the Holy Spirit. After they were baptized with the Holy Spirit, this same Peter stood up and persuaded three thousand people to become followers of Christ.

In the period following Peter's denial and before his baptism in the Holy Spirit, something occurred in his life. We read in the Gospel of John how Jesus Himself restored Peter:

> "So when they had eaten breakfast, Jesus said to Simon Peter, 'Simon, son of Jonah, do you love Me more than these?' He said to Him, 'Yes, Lord; You know that I love You.' He said to him, 'Feed My lambs.'
>
> He said to him again a second time, 'Simon, son of Jonah, do you love Me?' He said to Him, 'Yes, Lord; You know that I love You.' He said to him, 'Tend My sheep.'
>
> He said to him the third time, 'Simon, son of Jonah, do you love Me?' Peter was grieved because He said to him the third time, 'Do you love Me?' And he said to Him, 'Lord, You know all things; You know that I love You.' Jesus said to him, 'Feed My sheep'.

> ...And when He had spoken this, He said to him, 'Follow Me.'" (John 21:15-19, NKJ)

Restoration begins with God's forgiveness. I needed His forgiveness to cover me, just like the prayer shawl that my friend had given me, before He could anoint me fully with His Holy Spirit. I could not understand it. I thought that that was the reason why Jesus had died on the cross, not only for me, but also for all people throughout the ages. Forgiveness is one of the basic elements of Christianity. Why would I be struggling with the essence of Christianity nearly twenty years after giving my life to God? Did I not receive His forgiveness when His death on the cross became real to me? I have often felt like the apostle Paul, the worst of all sinners, yet I believed in God's forgiveness and that He had set me free from my sins.

A deeper study of Peter revealed that he had to acknowledge his sin before he could receive restoration. I looked at his sin.

> "But he (Peter) said to Him, 'Lord, I am ready to go with You, both to prison and to death.'
>
> Then He said, 'I tell you, Peter, the rooster shall not crow this day before you will deny three times that you know Me.'" (Luke 22: 33-34, NKJ)

> "Having arrested Him, they led Him and brought Him into the high priest's house. But Peter followed at a distance.
>
> Now when they had kindled a fire in the midst of the courtyard and sat down together, Peter sat among them.
>
> And a certain servant girl, seeing him as he sat by the fire, looked intently at him and said, 'This man was also with Him.'

> But he denied Him, saying, 'Woman, I do not know Him.'
>
> And after a little while another saw him and said, 'You also are of them.' But Peter said, 'Man, I am not!'
>
> Then after about an hour had passed, another confidently affirmed, saying, 'Surely this fellow also was with Him, for he is a Galilean.'
>
> But Peter said, 'Man, I do not know what you are saying!' Immediately, while he was still speaking, the rooster crowed.
>
> And the Lord turned and looked at Peter. Then Peter remembered the word of the Lord, how He had said to him, 'Before the rooster crows, you will deny Me three times.'
>
> So Peter went out and wept bitterly."
>
> (Luke 22:54-62, NKJ)

Peter was full of himself when he boasted that he would never leave or forsake Jesus. He needed to be shown that his flesh was sinful so that he could become a humble follower of Jesus Christ. After Peter's first and second verbal responses of denial, he had enough time to remember the promise made a few hours earlier to the Son of God. There was opportunity to acknowledge that he was a follower, that he loved Jesus and that he was prepared to die for Him. We read that an hour passed between his second and third denial. What went on in Peter's mind in that long hour? Why was his sin not too great an error to him? He knew he was denying the Lord, but coldheartedly he continued. He was warned by Jesus earlier that he was going to deny Him, therefore he had fore-knowledge in this matter. Instead of fulfilling his vows to Jesus, standing alongside his Friend, facing the physical and verbal abuse of the enemy, Peter was overcome by fear. And then lastly, his aggressive reaction showed no sign of remorse or guilt when denying Jesus. If that rooster had not crowed, he probably would have carried on denying Jesus to eternity.

It was the rooster crowing and the look of Jesus that broke Peter and turned him into a humble follower of Jesus Christ.

Peter in his own strength could not confess his sins. He needed a rooster and the Son of God before he could confess with weeping and sorrow. This heart-felt confession, his restoration and the baptism of the Holy Spirit changed Peter forever.

Instinctively I realized I too needed a rooster, a personal look from God and a mantle of fire.

I confronted my sins. With a shock I realized I had repented of my own sins in obedience, but not deeply from my heart like Peter. Whenever I met people, I would casually mention a sin or two of my past. I did not want them to think that I thought I was holy or without sin.

Peter was not like this. I cannot imagine him speaking to three thousand people telling them they should not worry about their sins because everyone sins. He himself also sinned in his past by denying the Son of God three times. I do not think Peter ever mentioned this sin again. This was a private matter between him and God. He wept bitterly, before Jesus forgave and restored him.

It became a daily habit, a ritual of mine to obediently ask for the forgiveness of all my sins. The focus was, however, on the forgiveness of Jesus and not on my repentance. The priority should have been a deep repenting of sins and then receiving the forgiveness of Jesus.

The second alarming revelation I received shattered my self-confidence. Somehow I was only looking at known, open, obvious sins. The dark secrets of my heart remained secret to me. I began to realize that I could not receive the forgiveness of Jesus to cover my sins, without exposing my heart to Him and more important to myself. I had to delve into the depths of my heart to dig out the hidden sins. I knew it would be for my sake. Jesus knew Peter was going to deny Him. Peter did not foresee it. After denying Jesus, it was in a sense not necessary to confess his sins to Jesus, but for his own sake, to realize he was a humble, weak sinner. Later, on the beach, when Peter declared that he loved Jesus, there was no boastful pledge he would follow Jesus to prison or death. The changed Peter now realized he was weak, humble and broken.

I was only slightly off the mark, but the truth is that I had missed the point. I confessed a forgiving Jesus, without a deep conviction of sins. Jesus is a forgiving God and this should be the central message of the gospel, however, we should firstly be aware of our sins, confess them and repent of them before we can receive forgiveness.

Could this be a mistake of the modern times we are living in? We focus on the forgiveness of Jesus. You only have to receive Him in your heart and then you become a child of God. Sunday after Sunday pastors ask people to accept Jesus in their hearts. We quickly ask for the forgiveness of our known sins and then Jesus jumps into our hearts. I love to pray for revival. People all over the world are seriously praying for revival. I know revival starts when God revives the individual.

Surely revival will begin when people will hear their own roosters crowing, see the look on Jesus' face, confront the sin in their hearts, weep bitterly, fall down on their faces in the presence of the living God, stop sinning and turn to God. Are we missing the repentance that John the Baptist preached, the basics of Christianity?

I certainly missed it. After Resje was born, I confessed with my lips that I led a sinful life, asking Jesus to change my life. But no rooster crowed and I never looked into Jesus' eyes. I never went outside and wept bitterly. I stopped committing the obvious sins, not daring to look into my dark, cold heart. I wanted to receive God's forgiveness without exposing my heart. Jesus knew I was naked and exposed. He knew about my sins before I committed them. I had to face them and be repulsed by them, not boast about them. I had serious homework to do.

The key for me was to have a deeper look at the facial expression of Jesus before I could go to Father God. When Jesus was about to raise Lazarus from the dead, He did not jump up and down with joy because He was going to perform one of His greatest miracles. He looked at the loved ones of Lazarus. He saw their tears and wept.

When the rooster crowed, Peter broke down. He lost all confidence in himself. He would never boast about his strength and his abilities again. Only hours before the crucifixion of Jesus, Peter became a broken man. The apostles, with Peter as their leader, could only now be empowered with the Holy Spirit to carry the ministry of Jesus into Jerusalem, Judea and Samaria and to the ends of the earth. Once again instead of expressing or showing His joy, Jesus looked at Peter and had utmost empathy with His beloved friend seeing and confronting his own inner being. Jesus knew how far He had to go to break Peter. In compelling Peter to look at his own heart, it did not only break Peter, it also broke Jesus. It broke Jesus to break His friend. And it was this look of sorrow and sympathy, of love and forgiveness, of pain and hurt, of naked rawness that caused Peter to run away, weeping bitterly and to appear on the beach broken but healed, a sinner but forgiven, an outcast but loved.

This is how Jesus was looking at me. With a broken heart He was constantly looking into my heart. He knew what it was going to cost me to break down. I was looking at my flesh and circumstances, my problems and life, my abilities and strengths, my likes and dislikes, my talents and education, the sins that I had given up and the duties I had performed for

God. There was a hidden sin in my heart. Jesus was waiting for me to look at myself, to break into pieces; only then His forgiveness and mantle of fire could come down on me. Jesus knew the real me. I kept sinning and like Peter was adamant not to give up on my sins.

I knew the day I would break down, Jesus would break down too – for my sake. I always knew Jesus had compassion for me. His sacrificial love was real. I had a problem with Father God. I knew Jesus told His disciples that He and the Father were one and if they looked at Him, they looked at the Father. But I only saw Jesus. Father God sent Jesus to come and pay for our sins. After so many years Father God was still high up in heaven. Jesus was in my heart and the Holy Spirit was there, albeit a stranger to me, but God Himself was on the other side of the Jordan.

Thorough self-examination made me aware of a rooster following me at a distance. What was this rooster? There were no obvious sins in my life. I was faithful to my husband. I worked hard. I did not gossip, nor did I visit any worldly places. I had not forsaken the assembly of the believers. I walked and talked with Jesus, like Peter. I followed Jesus, like Peter. I recognized His voice, sat at His feet, became alive in His presence.

When Jesus restored Peter, His instructions were clear. If Peter loved the Lord, he was to feed and tend to the other sheep. Peter stopped sinning openly when he chose to walk with Jesus; he admired and loved Him as a friend, obeying Him, yet he did not have the same love as Jesus in his heart till after the third denial. If Peter truly loved Jesus with all his power, might and strength, the way Jesus loves us, he would not have forsaken Jesus in His hour of trial. Peter understood that God was going to crown Jesus as the new earthly King. I wondered if Peter struggled like me, with the concept of how a loving God could forsake His own Son and turn Him into a public spectacle. Could that be the reason why he denied Jesus?

The rooster crowed loud and clear in my ears.

I did not love God. There was no love in my heart for God. I served Him, I remained faithful to Him, I knew Him, I followed Him…however, there was no love in my heart for Him. I loved Jesus, the Son of God and the Man I had got to know so well. But Jesus was the Son of God, not God the Father. My dark secret was, that although I sacrificed Resje, I still loved her more than I loved God. There was nothing I could do about that. It was wrong. God wanted to be loved more, and I could not do it. I did not want to love Him more than I loved Resje. I wanted to love Resje more. This was my hidden sin.

I knew I had reached the innermost part of my heart. The issue all along was love.

There was a hidden agenda in my search for God, hidden for me too, but when the rooster crowed it revealed to me the darkness, the hidden sins, the falseness and coldness of my heart. He knew this all along. I thought if I knew and followed Him, He might turn around and heal my daughter. Subconsciously I hoped that He would repay me if I spent all this time with Him, doing me a favour in return by healing my daughter. That was my reason for getting close to Jesus, for sacrificing Resje and for becoming involved with the God of the Universe.

I wanted something from God. I wanted Him to heal Resje.

Because He did not heal her, I did not love Him. Because He did not do what I asked Him to do, my heart grew cold towards Him. In refusing my request, He became a strong, powerful and hard taskmaster, so I built walls of protection and resistance around my heart.

I had to say that out loud to God. This was the sin that He wanted me to confess, to repent of and to turn away from. My heart was cold and hard, filthy and false, black and full of sins. I could not believe what I saw in my own heart. After serving Him all my life and being born again for nearly twenty years Father God received a cold heart from me. Together with this shocking realization, the knowledge came that I would never be able to change my heart by myself. To change, I needed Him to look upon me the way He had looked upon Peter. How would the God of the universe force me to love Him? How would He change my heart? Would He then be the God of the free choice that I got to know? Did He want me to do it?

Together with Elizabeth Barrett Browning I asked, "How do I love Thee?" I confessed while sobbing my heart out under my prayer shawl: "I love Thee not. There are no ways to count my love for Thee. I blame Thee … And what is more, I do not believe in Your love, I do not think You love me and I do not think You love Resje."

I searched for the reasons why I saw God the Father as unloving. Although I had a wonderful earthly father, I only realized his love and goodness after Resje was born. During my childhood years, my father never fulfilled the yearning of my heart. My earthly father was always there but I did not perceive him as wanting to be involved with me. I thought Father God was like that.

Later, the men I dated failed me. I thought their love would lift me up to higher levels of existence but I always came tumbling down. I thought Father God was like them.

Then I gave God one more chance when I became aware that I needed Him. When Resje was born I thought a powerful Father would love Resje so much that He would heal her. He did not and I closed my heart to Him.

I had the freedom to leave Him anytime, however I knew He held the keys to everlasting life. I chose to follow Him, but it was out of a sense of duty. I could not see His love for us by not responding to our requests. I saw the fact that He did not heal Resje as a punishment. He vented His anger on Resje. In my twisted mind, it felt like it was I who deserved punishment and in a demented way, I felt that maybe even Resje deserved punishment because of generational curses and iniquities. That was how I perceived God. That was the God that I followed and served. Because I did not receive His love, I could not love Him. Because I was under the impression that His heart was furious towards us, my heart was cold towards Him. I served Him because I thought He was angry with us. Then I thought once His anger subsided, He would heal Resje.

I had to rephrase the question asked by Elizabeth Barrett Browning. I had to find out from God the Father: How much do You love me?

I prayed Paul's prayer: *Father God, God of our Lord Jesus Christ, Father of glory, give me the spirit of wisdom and revelation, so that I may know you better. Enlighten the eyes of my heart that I may know the hope to which You have called me, the riches of Your glorious inheritance in the saints and the greatness of Your power for me who believes. I pray that You will strengthen me with power through Your Spirit in my inner being, so that Christ may dwell in my heart through faith. I pray that I will be rooted and established in love and that I will have power, together with all the saints, to grasp how wide and long and high and deep the love of Christ is and to know this love that surpasses knowledge so that I will be filled to the measure of all the fullness of God.*

(Ephesians 1: 17-19 and 3:16-19)

I always knew there was a reason for the Old Testament. I went there in search of the Father's love. As the Book of Job had brought me comfort in coping with Resje's suffering, I found the Father's love in Hosea.

> "Therefore, behold, I will allure her, will bring her into the wilderness, and speak comfort to her.
>
> I will give her her vineyards from there, and the Valley of Achor as a door of hope; she shall sing there, as in the days of her youth, as in the day when she came up from the land of Egypt.
>
> And it shall be, in that day, says the Lord that you will call Me 'My Husband' and no longer call Me 'My Master.'" (Hosea 2:14-16, NKJ)

The Valley of Achor in Hosea 2:15 refers to Joshua and the sins of Israel. Achor means, "trouble". After the Israelites invaded Jericho, Joshua warned them not to take from the accursed things so that they would not "make the camp of Israel a curse, and trouble it" (Joshua 6:18, NKJ). Achan took a Babylonian garment, two hundred shekels of silver and a wedge of gold and hid it in the earth in the midst of his tent, causing Israel's defeat at Ai. Joshua mourned God's absence and blessing by tearing his clothes, falling on his face and lamented:

> "Alas, Lord God, why have You brought this people over the Jordan at all – to deliver us into the hand of the Amorites, to destroy us? Oh, that we had been content, and dwelt on the other side of the Jordan!
>
> O Lord, what shall I say when Israel turns its back before its enemies?
>
> For the Canaanites and all the inhabitants of the land will hear it, and surround us, and cut off our name from the earth. Then what will You do for Your great name?" (Joshua 7:7-9, NKJ)

God impatiently answered Joshua:

> "Get up, sanctify the people, and say, Sanctify yourselves for tomorrow, because thus says the Lord God of Israel: There is an accursed thing in your midst, O Israel; you cannot stand before your enemies until you take away the accursed thing from among you." (Joshua 7:13, NKJ)

Once they had stoned and burned the guilty sinner, the Lord turned from the fierceness of His anger. Nowadays we do not have to be stoned and burned. Jesus was crucified for our sins in our place. But we still need to dig up the sins we buried in our tents/hearts and bring them before God.

Was this the reason why I could not stand before my enemies? This accursed sin of mine, my unloving heart, prevented God from giving us the victory over our enemies. According to Jesus the most important commandment of them all, is to love God. I was worshipping and serving God, praying to Him, yet not obeying His Commandments. The crowing rooster revealed the magnitude of my sin. Once I heard the rooster, it would not stop crowing. As I was about to give up completely, I realized the rooster did not only reveal my sins to myself – it also brought the new daylight with him. Dawn was breaking. The rooster, in fact, announced the end of a long, dark night. The sun was not yet shining, but I could see the streaks of dawn. I still needed God's look before I could weep bitterly. I had already seen the look on Jesus' face. I needed to see the face of Father God, something that not even Moses was allowed to see.

Once again I had to go back to the foundations. This time it was faith that I needed. I needed to believe that the words of God were true. I needed the faith of a child. I needed to believe that God loved me.

God's Kingdom works in strange ways. He was promising me vineyards in the wilderness and a door of hope in my Valley of Achor. In real life you do not find vineyards in the wilderness, neither can hope arise from trouble. Yet God was saying that to me. He was saying that if I believed this He would then become a husband to me. I would understand His love, the way a husband loves his wife. God functions in the opposite of what we expect. We want to be prosperous, healthy, rich and famous. Jesus says:

> "Blessed are the poor in spirit, for theirs is the kingdom of heaven.
>
> Blessed are those who mourn, for they shall be comforted.
>
> Blessed are the meek, for they shall inherit the earth.
>
> Blessed are those who hunger and thirst for righteousness, for they shall be filled."
>
> (Matthew 5:3-6, NKJ)

We want to enter into God's presence, proud to be His sons and daughters, ruling as heirs; Jesus taught us humility in God's Kingdom by washing the feet of His friends.

As future rulers we want to stand up straight; in God's Kingdom, we need to kneel down in prayer.

We want to live in this world as people of this world; Jesus says:

> "If you were of the world, the world would love its own. Yet because you are not of the world, but I chose you out of the world, therefore the world hates you." (John 15:19, NKJ)

We want to care for our lives; in God's Kingdom Jesus says we have to crucify ourselves.

I went back to my first disappointment in God, when I was seven years old and the doctor, not Jesus, removed the splinter from my nail. The doctor even enhanced the absence of Jesus when he said, "Dear Jesus is not here, I am!" I tried to look at this situation crucifying my thoughts and ideas, opening myself to the unseen. As a little girl, I prayed to Jesus to remove the splinter… and the splinter was removed, not the way I wanted it to be done, but we should always pray according to God's will, not our own. Looking at it with the eyes of my heart, I realized that Jesus had removed that splinter from my nail. He used the doctor's hands and expertise to do it. The doctor was the instrument in God's hands that day. I had prayed and God had answered. He had sent somebody who could remove the splinter. Jesus was indeed there! The doctor was wrong. If he had known then what I know now, the doctor could have been the perfect likeness of Jesus to a young child. Oh, how the doctor would have lived differently if he only had given the glory to God that He deserved. I did not understand how God worked, neither did the doctor.

It was easy for me to believe in the unseen because the doctor helped me. Something positive came out of all this – the splinter was removed. The next step was to believe in the goodness of a God who loves you when you see or experience pain, death and suffering. If I could discover this truth, then maybe God would turn His face towards me and I would be able to look Him in the eyes, the eyes of perfect love.

I did not know where to start. I thought of the words of Jesus:
> "I and My Father are one." (John 10:30, NKJ)

> "… though you do not believe Me, believe the works, that you may know and believe that the Father is in Me, and I in Him." (John 10:38, NKJ)

> "If you had known Me, you would have known My Father also." (John 8:19b, NKJ)

I knew these truths so well in my mind. But my heart could not believe in a loving Father. He stayed in heaven, while His Son had to do all the work. I went to my motherly heart and I discovered there something of the Fatherly heart.

The worst thing in my life was to see my daughter suffer. I felt completely powerless because I could not take her pain away. If only I could put the giant pigmented naevi on myself or give her my skin. If it were medically possible, I would have given her all my skin. They could take my life any moment and give her a life free of suffering. Helping her cope with the itching and the scratching was not enough; I wanted to remove it completely. To see her suffer was worse to me than to have suffered in her place. I watched helplessly as she experienced her own hell, powerless to heal her.

The doors of my heart slowly opened to Father God when I realized that He could identify with me. He had been in the same position as everyone who'd ever gazed upon the face of suffering. He watched His Son's suffering. He did not send angels to help His own Son, or put out His own hands to receive the nails. He had to send His own Son into hell to go snatch the keys of Hades and of death from the hands of the devil himself. He understood my feelings of powerlessness. He knew exactly what I was going through every time I looked upon the suffering of my daughter. He knew my thoughts and my desires. He could identify with me. My frozen heart slowly started melting.

Every time I expressed my heartfelt desire to take Resje's suffering away from her, she would try to comfort me by saying: "No, Mommy, Jesus made me strong. You would never be able to carry this. God made my body stronger than this giant pigmented naevi."

I went back to the Son to hear what He was saying about His Father:

> "Most assuredly, I say to you, Moses did not give you the bread from heaven, but My Father gives you the true bread from heaven.
>
> For the bread of God is He who comes down from heaven and gives life to the world."
>
> (John 6:32-33, NKJ)
>
> "For I have come down from heaven, not to do My own will, but the will of Him who sent Me.
>
> This is the will of the Father who sent Me, that of all He has given Me I should lose nothing, but should raise it up at the last day." (John 6:38-39, NKJ)

These words penetrated my heart. God had to break His Son into broken bread. Whereas Resje was my broken daughter, Jesus was the broken Son of God. Like the manna that fell from the heavens, Jesus was poured out onto the earth. Father God wanted to give me life and the true bread from heaven. He wanted to feed me to keep me alive. He did not want to lose me. He wanted to raise me up on the last day to sit with Him in the Heavenly Places; therefore, for the sake of giving me everlasting life, He broke His Son.

Father God was starting to turn His head in my direction to look at me. Or maybe I was the one turning into the right direction to find Him standing there, in the same spot He has been standing since the beginning of creation, looking, looking at me.

Instead of paying our way, or working like slaves, to enter into God's Kingdom, God chose a method no one would expect of Him. He chose to break His own Son into pieces so that we could eat from the heavenly bread and live.

Oh, how I wanted to see God's face! I searched everywhere. I found the following two truths:

> "No one has seen God at any time. The only begotten Son, who is in the bosom of the Father, He has declared Him." (John 1:18, NKJ)

The Son is in the bosom of the Father. Jesus is the heart of God! Father God in His love for us, had actually ripped out His own heart, broke it into pieces and threw it out on earth. That emphasized the cost of God's love for us.

The second truth simply stated that I was asking something unattainable. No one has ever seen God. God confirmed it when He said to His friend, Moses:

> "You cannot see My face; for no man shall see Me, and live." (Exodus 33:20, NKJ)

Moses begged God to show him His glory. Eventually God agreed, hiding Moses in a cleft in a rock to show him His glory. Like John in the Book of Revelation, who turned around looking for the Lion of Judah only to find the slain Lamb, the same thing happened. God did not show Moses His face, His Magnificence, Power or Majesty. He showed Moses His back. God's back was God's glory. It was the beaten, torn, bloody back of Jesus that Moses saw. He saw God's vulnerability, His brokenness and suffering. Salvation came to mankind through pain and suffering. The suffering of God was His glory.

I had to accept that I was not going to see God's face. Through Jesus I have seen the heart of God. This was better than His face.

When the rooster crowed and Jesus turned to look at Peter, Jesus at that moment identified with Peter. At the same moment that Jesus was breaking Peter, Father God was breaking Jesus into bread.

To make wine, you have to crush grapes. God was crushing His own heart. Blood came pouring out. That blood turned into wine for us, to celebrate everlasting life. The look on Jesus' face was of pain and sorrow. It was a picture of God's heart breaking.

I saw in my mind how the veil of the temple was torn in two and although God sent darkness to cover the earth so that no one could see His face while Jesus was dying on the cross, I had a glimpse. Like my tears for Resje, I saw the tears of Almighty God rolling down and heard Him roar like a wounded lion, tearing the earth, cleaving apart the mountainous rocks.

He was a heart-broken Father. He gave His Son as a gift to the world so that Jesus could become the Son of Man. God then had to look upon mankind He created and see how they despised, hated and killed His gift to them. I had always thought the darkness that God sent was because He could no longer look upon the suffering of His Son. Now I realized it was also because He could no longer look upon the hatred of His children.

Jesus turned His face to look at me - pain and sorrow pouring out of His eyes. Time stood still. Slowly I looked back.

Did it take Resje's suffering to break me?

Did God know that it would require all this suffering of Resje before I would become broken? Did the look on Jesus' face say how sorry He was that Father God had to go this far before I would humble myself? Did God give me this little girl out of love? Did He love me so much that He would use everything in order for me to one day be in His presence? Was Resje's pain and suffering His way of showing me His love?

I shook my head. I could never believe this. And even if I did by some obscurity, how would I ever convince Resje that her pain and suffering is a sign of God's love? Father God would never go this far. It was too much for me. Who would follow a God who gives us pain and suffering because He loves us? Who would read this and not want to stop serving a God who lavishes us with hurt? How could I make sense of this? How could Resje and all the other people who suffer understand this concept? Were the tumours on Resje's skin, the arms of God around me? This was absurd. This was totally wrong. I thought I had lost it.

I asked Him directly:

Did You give Resje this cursed condition because You love me and want me closer to You?

He answered:
> "Everyone who is called by My name, whom I have created for My glory; I have formed him, yes, I have made him." (Isaiah 43:7, NKJ)

What have You done, Father God?

> "Behold, I have refined you, but not as silver; I have tested you in the furnace of affliction."
> (Isaiah 48:10, NKJ)

Why have You done this, Father God?

> "Lift up your eyes to the heavens, and look on the earth beneath. For the heavens will vanish away like smoke, the earth will grow old like a garment, and those who dwell in it will die in like manner; but My salvation will be forever, and My righteousness will not be abolished." (Isaiah 51:6, NKJ)

What about my little girl, Lord? Where is Your love for her?

> "Can a woman forget her nursing child, and not have compassion on the (daughter) of her womb? Surely they may forget, yet I will not forget (her). See, I have inscribed (her) on the palms of My hands."
>
> (Isaiah 49:15-16, NKJ)

I needed someone to comfort me. My desire was for my father and mother who would have comforted and prayed with me without asking any questions. My father had died when Resje was nine years old and my mother was on the other side of the Jordan, in Johannesburg. God took care of my longing:

> "I, even I am He who comforts you".
>
> (Isaiah 51:12, NKJ)

I feel so ashamed, Lord God.

> "For you will forget the shame of your youth, and will not remember the reproach of your widowhood anymore.
>
> For your Maker is your husband, the Lord of hosts is His name; and your Redeemer is the Holy One of Israel; He is called the God of the whole earth."

(Isaiah 54:4b-5)

"For a mere moment I have forsaken you, but with great mercies I will gather you. With a little wrath I hid My face from you for a moment; but with everlasting kindness I will have mercy on you."

(Isaiah 54:7-8, NKJ)

Was this true that God knew the only way I could feel His touch was through the suffering of my daughter?

This question might imply that God caused Resje to be born like this. We would like to believe that sickness is from the devil and that God wants us all to be healthy and fit. I would really like to believe that too.

The disciples asked Jesus who healed a man born blind if it was the sins of this man or the sins of the man's parents that were the cause of his blindness. Jesus answered:

"Neither this man nor his parents sinned, but that the works of God should be revealed in him."

(John 9:3, NKJ)

In this case, the devil did not cause the blindness.

In another example Jesus said:

"Unless you people see signs and wonders, you will by no means believe." (John 4:48, NKJ)

Could it be that there were a few illnesses and deformities that were amongst the people so that Jesus could heal them and that the miraculous healing was then a sign for people to believe?

Why did Jesus deliberately wait until Lazarus was dead before He went to Bethany? He clearly did not only want to restore Lazarus to health, but also to life, giving God all the honour and glory as a Healer and Resurrector of the dead.

How do we understand the meaning of the following scriptures?

> "Now see that I, even I, am He, and there is no God besides Me; I kill and I make alive; I wound and I heal…" (Deuteronomy 32:39, NKJ);

> "Come, and let us return to the Lord; for He has torn, but He will heal us; He has stricken, but He will bind us up." (Hosea 6:1, NKJ)

Because of the prayers of my parents, God wanted me to sit with Him in the Heavenlies. I could not get there by myself. In His mercy and love God chose Resje to become an instrument of suffering. To save me, He could not heal Resje at once. He cried with me and with Resje. However, He looked beyond this world of pain and suffering and saw how the Heavenlies were slowly opening up for us. He saw the joy of spending eternity with the two of us. That was the meaning of Resje's suffering. We were slowly dying to the life we thought we could have, a life filled with laughter, no pain and a healthy skin. While we were dying, the heavens opened up for us, revealing a life glittering with jewels and joy, love and peace.

Resje was chosen to bring glory to God. I saw her back. I saw her torture, her suffering and pain, her agony and brokenness. And the everlasting life of God flowed through me. Her back showed me the glory of God.

As God said in Hosea He allured me out of my world into the wilderness of suffering. The trouble of my sinful life became a door of hope of spending eternity with Him. This is the day that I will call Him my Husband and no longer my Master. If I close my eyes for a minute I can see Him as a husband in love, sacrificing everything for His lover.

Yes, Lord, this makes my heart want to sing, but the notes stick in my throat at the thought of Resje's suffering and sacrifice. She had to sacrifice her health in order for her mother to have eternal life. The day You show me Your love for her, is the day I will call you my Husband.

'Look at all the things I have given her: parents who love her and care for her; doctors and nurses who help her; My broken Son for her to feed on; My Holy Spirit to give her all the power she needs; a ministry that one day she will take up and run with; authority over the works of the devil; a special place in My Kingdom; many souls to bring to salvation and I can go on and on. You must remember that she was conceived in my heart long before she was conceived in your womb.'

One thing she needs, God. Why do You not include her healing in the outpouring of Your love?

'I want you to love me for who I am, not for healing your daughter.'

His words penetrated the depths of my soul. The look of love and forgiveness went to the very core of my heart where everything revolved around Resje's healing. I needed to love God because of Him, not because of what I hoped He would do for Resje. Even though I had sacrificed her years ago, Resje still sat on the throne of my heart. God was not God in His own right in my life. He was the God who could heal Resje. Because He did not heal her, I could not love Him.

I had to reach the place where Habakkuk could say to God:

> "Though the fig tree may not blossom, nor fruit be on the vines; though the labor of the olive may fail, and the fields yield no food; though the flock may be cut off from the fold, and there be no herd in the stalls - Yet I will rejoice in the Lord, I will joy in the God of my salvation." (Habakkuk 3:17-18, NKJ)

I heard the rooster and saw the look of love and forgiveness on the face of Jesus and in the heart of Father God. I was convicted, confessed my sins, wept bitterly and received His love. I now knew the sin in my heart; yet, I could not rip it out. I thought that I had ripped it out years ago on a farm in Zimbabwe when I had sacrificed her in my desire for her healing. Now the falseness of my motives was exposed. I had thought God would heal her if I sacrificed her.

My heart ached with longing to be on the other side of the Jordan, feasting with the others. I sat down on the floodplain, looking at the waters rising steadily. I had my friend's prayer shawl wrapped around me. I knew before I could cross the Jordan I would have to rip my heart out the way God had ripped His heart out to give us Jesus. He could do it because He was God. I was a mere human being, a weak woman.

My flesh wanted to remain sitting, waiting to drown. I looked at the other side and had a glimpse of a Husband waiting for His bride to enter the church before the wedding ceremony could take place. Together with the wedding ring He had precious gems in His pocket: diamonds, sapphires, rubies, pearls. I remained sitting. What were jewels to me if I was to drown? I would give all the jewels in the world for my daughter to be healed. I was not even dressed in a wedding gown, barefoot, covered in mud. He looked at me, put the jewels back and with His Hand in the other pocket took out a handkerchief. I stared at the white handkerchief. He motioned to me. He was waiting for me to rip out my heart; then He would wipe away my tears.

I clutched my fingers around my heart, trying to delve into my flesh but my fingers were not strong enough to tear it open. I looked up. In front of me, the floodplain of the Jordan stretched endlessly.

Chapter Seven

A SOUND FROM HEAVEN

When queen Jezebel vowed that she was going to kill Elijah in the same manner he had killed her Baal prophets, he fled. We read the following:

> "But he (Elijah) himself went a day's journey into the wilderness, and came and sat down under a broom tree. And he prayed that he might die, and said, 'It is enough! Now, Lord, take my life, for I am no better than my fathers!'
>
> Then as he lay and slept under a broom tree, suddenly an angel touched him, and said to him, 'Arise and eat.'"
>
> (1 Kings 19:4-5, NKJ)
>
> "So he arose, and ate and drank; and he went in the strength of that food forty days and forty nights as far as Horeb, the mountain of God.
>
> And there he went into a cave, and spent the night in that place; and behold, the word of the Lord came to him and He said to him, 'What are you doing here, Elijah?'
>
> So he said, 'I have been very zealous for the Lord God of hosts; for the children of Israel have forsaken Your covenant, torn down Your altars, and killed Your

> prophets with the sword. I alone am left; and they seek to take my life.'
>
> Then He said, 'Go out, and stand on the mountain before the Lord.' And behold, the Lord passed by..."
>
> (1 Kings 19:8-11, NKJ)

I reached Elijah's broom tree. I had reasoned with God and tried to understand His ways. It was enough. I knew that I was not better than anyone else and had exhausted my reserves. This was the moment where I had to bow down to the King of Kings and say to Him, 'Not my will be done in Resje's life, but Yours'. I took her out of His arms when He did not heal her or relieve her agony, pressing her so hard against my chest that she slipped into my heart to take His place. He was waiting for me to give her back to Him.

As confirmation a dear friend bought me a gift in Australia. God told her to buy it for me. It was a set of two butterfly brooches. She simply said God told her the time had come for me to let go of Resje. A baby butterfly was attached to the wings of the first butterfly. The second brooch was the baby butterfly by itself, grown-up in all her splendour. She was free from her mother. She had exactly the same DNA as her mother but instead of clinging to her mother, three beautiful glittering stars were attached to her gorgeous sparkling wings, signifying God the Father, Jesus the Son and the Holy Spirit.

Through tears I knew what I had to do. Resje belonged to God. He would take care of her for the rest of her life. I carried her, but God wanted her to be free. He loved her more than I ever could. With His love came forgiveness, salvation, freedom, healing, restoration, eternal life and blessing upon blessing. Most importantly if I give her to Him, I would be free from carrying this burden and He would enter the sacred place in my heart to become my Lover and Husband. He was waiting for me. I knew He was not going to rip out my heart for me. He wanted me to do it. He was asking me to trust Him with the person I loved the most in the entire world.

Trusting God for our salvation and everlasting life was not difficult for me. I could not always understand God, but I always trusted His promise of eternal life. I found it difficult though to trust God with Resje's medical condition. I had seen Him repeatedly turning His back on our requests. We were begging Him daily to relieve Resje of the itching, blessing her with a new skin. He was denying our requests daily. It was as if God refused to help her or to make it easier for her. How could I give her over to Him? What would He do to her?

There were two routes to take. Could it be that the devil had some power over this and that I had to stand up against the powers of darkness? That is what happened to Job. We are warned:

> "For we do not wrestle against flesh and blood, but against principalities, against powers, against the rulers of the darkness of this age, against spiritual hosts of wickedness in the heavenly places."

(Ephesians 6:12, NKJ)

The second route was to submit to God. In my struggling walk with God I had come to the point where I needed to exchange Resje's place in my heart with God's. There was nothing to discuss about this matter. I simply had to do it.

Both routes were leading to the top of Mount Horeb, where God wanted me to stand and wait for Him to come down.

I knew for sure that God would come down from heaven once I had reached the top, that He would turn the prayer shawl my friend had given me into Elijah's mantle and that I would be able to strike the waters of the Jordan River. Once Elisha crossed the River Jordan with Elijah's mantle, he stayed in

Jericho. The men of the city told him that the water was bad and the ground barren. Elisha threw salt into the source, proclaiming God's healing over the water, with no more death or barrenness as a result (2 Kings 2:19-22). There were so many people in my life across the River Jordan that needed salt. I knew what life and fruitfulness would mean to them by the power of the Holy Spirit. God was urging me on.

It was a high mountain, the top stretched endlessly into the heavens. It was not because I was confused that I did not know which route to take. I was simply exhausted. I needed some food to regain my strength.

I looked for someone being formed into the likeness of Jesus Christ to help me. I found none. Surely at least one person in my life should have been able to give me something to eat. I waited for God to send me an angel.

I wondered why people would hide Jesus and the power of the Holy Spirit if God were living within their hearts. Could it be that we hide Jesus because we do not want Him to arise in our lives? We want to hold on to our own little kingdoms where we are on the thrones of our lives. We want to decide what to do with people. Do we like them? Do we want to get to know them better? We only accept people who are like us, who have the same tastes, the same interests and the same lifestyle. Jesus embarrasses us with His love and His kindness, His forgiveness and acceptance He has for all people. We want to be exclusive. We act as if Jesus only died for people like us. As soon as a sinner gives his life over to God, we train him to become like us. We do not go out to the world to change people; the odd saved person needs to come to us.

We are neither filled with the power of the Holy Spirit so that God can do miraculous healings through us, nor are we anointed children of God for Him to reach out to the lost and the broken, the sick and the hurt. We have lost the power of the first New Testament church because we are standing in the way of the Holy Spirit. We have not died to ourselves so that

Jesus Christ can rise up in our lives. We are neither cold nor hot, but lukewarm and in the process have lost a vibrant victorious life.

This is the reason why I needed an angel to give me food. I could not find ten Spirit-filled Christians, not five, not even one who could give me of the food I was looking for. They were all in the same spiritual state as I. We walk the walk and we talk the talk without God's power or anointing.

I had to deal with my flesh, my heart. God told me through Moses:
> "Therefore circumcise the foreskin of your heart, and be stiff-necked no longer." (Deuteronomy 10:16, NKJ)

It is a painful operation – the circumcision of one's heart. Like many followers of Jesus I could have turned away. After Jesus explained to His followers that they needed to eat and drink His flesh and blood many of his followers were offended:
> "From that time many of His disciples went back and walked with Him no more." (John 6:66, NKJ)

When Jesus asked the twelve if they also wanted to leave, Simon Peter answered Him:
> "Lord, to whom shall we go? You have the words of eternal life." (John 6:68, NKJ)

Many of Jesus' followers accepted and benefited from His healing ministry. It was marvelous to see Jesus in action: Water turned to wine, the sick healed, the dead raised and food freely distributed to everyone. It is the same today. Many people accept Jesus as part of their lives. He becomes a super hero when He heals and forgives and dies for us. He is welcome to come into our homes to live with us. At first Jesus asks little. He wants us to listen and obey, to stop sinning and start caring for others. Some of us do this willingly, some maybe not that willingly, but we all try and struggle and by the grace of God manage to live a mediocre Christian life.

It was when Jesus explained His principles about brokenness to His followers that it became too hard to follow Him. He warns us that our flesh is no good, in fact it is useless or to be more precise it is a hindrance in our walk with Him. We need to deny ourselves, crucify our flesh, circumcise our hearts and become as broken and bloody as He was. This is extremely difficult. Nobody wants to be broken. We want exactly the opposite, to be whole and wholesome.

There is an unending account of the struggles and battles of the Israelites in the Old Testament. They knew God existed, but they tried to lead their lives in their own flesh, generation after generation. God had to intervene. In His infinite wisdom He knew that they were never going to make it in their own flesh, therefore He sent His own Son to pay for our sins and then sent us a Helper to lead the way.

I was not strong or clever enough to cross the Jordan in my own strength or to circumcise my own heart. I reached a point where I recognized I must either walk away like the followers of Jesus, or accept the teaching of Jesus on suffering.

Before Resje was born I was living in bondage in my Egypt, serving the wicked king of the world:

> "…because the Lord loves you, and because He would keep the oath which He swore to your fathers, the Lord has brought you out with a mighty hand, and redeemed you from the house of bondage, from the hand of Pharaoh king of Egypt."
>
> (Deuteronomy 7:8, NKJ)

Painfully I died to my past life with all my dreams and desires. Like the Israelites, I never rejoiced or thanked Him that He saved me from the house of bondage. I complained and got angry with God, longing for the meat and the lifestyle of Egypt.

God then intervened. In His infinite wisdom and love He had to explain to me His principles of brokenness. It took me a long time to understand. He illustrated it through the suffering of my daughter. While the doctors were peeling off her skin, God was peeling away my flesh.

The pain and trauma made me aware of my position. I was living in the wilderness under the agonizing heat of the sun. With my reasoning I was going round and round in circles. My legs were extremely tired from this long journey - I could barely walk.

Then one day, by the grace of God, He lifted my head, called out to me, "Talitha, cumi!" and eventually succeeded in shifting my focus to the Promised Land.

There was the Promised Land, full of milk and honey, beckoning me to cross over.

It became clear to me that I had to die to my flesh in the desert for Him to raise me up and fill me with His Spirit so that I could live. It is when you die to yourself, that Jesus Christ is raised in your spirit. Once Jesus Christ is raised, you portray the image of Jesus to other people. Your own ears die to the importance of your own wants and the ears of Jesus inside you open to other people's needs. Your physical eyes close to your own views and interests and the spiritual eyes of Jesus Christ within you open to the souls of others. Your own heart stops beating for yourself, and the heart of Jesus opens to the desires of other people. Your own arms stop hugging yourself, and the arms of Jesus Christ open to invite people into your world. You with your own worldview and preconceived ideas, your likes and dislikes, your preferences and personal tastes do not exist anymore. It is Jesus within you that wants to reach out to the people you meet. Some need salvation, others healing; some people need encouragement, others a friend; some need someone to talk to, others life and hope.

Once we die to our fleshly desires, we become broken bread. The Spirit of the living God then fills you and it is the Spirit that gives life and that life is eternal. Jesus said:

> "It is the Spirit who gives life; the flesh profits nothing. The words that I speak to you are spirit, and they are life." (John 6:63, NKJ)

The angel gave food to Elijah; we can give food to people to feed on.

It was an enormous relief the day I realized I could not serve God with my flesh. My intelligence, talents and deeds profited nothing. It did not bring me closer in my relationship with God. I could reason with God for another twenty years, it was not going to bring me anywhere.

I searched His Word, looking for ways how to get to the top of Mount Horeb. One day while I was studying the Bible, I skipped a meal, realizing His Word was giving me food, like the angel giving food to Elijah. I threw my arms in the air. An angel touched me! His Word was the food that I needed to grow strong. The Bible was my angel! I jumped for joy, kneeling and crying. I looked up at Mount Horeb. Somehow it did not look that high anymore.

I had a few more pleasant surprises. The same book in the Bible that brought me the curses I thought we lived under after Resje was born brought me life. Almost twenty years later I discovered God's presence a mere three chapters after the curses:

> "Then Moses went and spoke these words to all Israel.
>
> And he said to them: 'I am one hundred and twenty years old today. I can no longer go out and come in. Also the Lord has said to me, "You shall not cross over this Jordan."
>
> 'The Lord your God Himself crosses over before you; He will destroy these nations from before you and you shall dispossess them.'" (Deuteronomy 31:1-3, NKJ)

> "'Be strong and of good courage, do not fear nor be afraid of them; for the Lord your God, He is the One who goes with you. He will not leave you nor forsake you.'
>
> Then Moses called Joshua and said to him in the sight of all Israel, 'Be strong and of good courage, for you must go with this people to the land which the Lord has sworn to their fathers to give them, and you shall cause them to inherit it.
>
> And the Lord, He is the One who goes before you. He will be with you, He will not leave you nor forsake you; do not fear nor be dismayed.'"
>
> (Deuteronomy 31:6-8 NKJ)

It sounded so easy, nearly too easy. God did not want me to cross the Jordan by myself. He Himself was crossing before me. I only needed to follow Him. Previously my main task had been to cross the Jordan, now I was looking further ahead at the Promised Land that was waiting on the other side. The land was inviting and lively, it took away the fear of the life-threatening river.

I found another wonderful surprise in Deuteronomy.

> "And the Lord your God will circumcise your heart and the heart of your descendants, to love the Lord your God with all your heart and with all your soul, that you may live." (Deuteronomy 30:6, NKJ)

Resje was the foreskin around my heart. I thought I had to cut her away, performing my own circumcision. Now a gracious and loving God reached out to me, promising He would do the circumcision. I have read of strong mothers who give birth by themselves and need to cut their own umbilical cords. I was not that strong, the doctor had to cut the physical cord when she was born. Now the heavenly Doctor was telling me that the time had come to let Him cut away the foreskin around my heart. I did not want to argue or reason with God, or try to understand His ways anymore. I had come a long way, the Promised Land was in front of me and there was no desire to go back into the wilderness. God's ways were better than mine. I submitted to Him and was humbled by Father God who offered to do this task. Yet, I needed to understand what happened between Resje and me. How did she become the foreskin of my heart? What happened in the period between an unwanted pregnancy to the present where I did not want to give her up?

God conceives us in His heart and then He looks for a suitable source on earth to give us the breath of life when we are born. Our lungs fill with oxygen and we begin living an earthly life. From the moment of birth the roles reverse. God then desires for us to conceive Him in our hearts, to give Him life when we are born again so that He can live an earthly life in our bodies. It is when He lives in us that we can reach out to other people, heal the sick, raise the dead, turn water into wine, become broken bread for the hungry. Our hearts become His dwelling place, His temple.

Jesus once got upset and overturned the tables of the people conducting worldly business in God's temple:

> "…It is written, My house shall be called a house of prayer, but you have made it a den of thieves."
>
> (Matthew 21:13, NKJ)

In the very next verse we read what happened the moment the temple was cleared of the corrupt merchants:

> "Then the blind and the lame came to Him in the temple, and He healed them". (Matthew 21:14, NKJ)

When Resje was born with her skin condition I closed my heart. God kept knocking at the door of my heart. To prevent listening to Him, I put Resje in front of my heart. My broken heart had to be protected. Resje became the foreskin of my heart, to protect and guard my heart and to prevent God from slipping in, or touching my heart. This of course was not a deliberate, conscious or planned decision. It happened subconsciously, without me knowing what was going on.

In the meantime I was begging God to perform a miracle, accusing Him of turning away, angry with Him for ignoring us. Because He was not living in my heart, I could not lean on Him for strength. I could not carry this burden by myself, I needed a crutch to lean on. Resje's suffering became my crutch. She and her suffering or to put it in a more positive way, my desire for her healing, became my crutch. No God or anything else in this world could touch my heart. Resje, my foreskin, was wrapped all around it.

I did not want to give her to God because I did not trust Him with her, so I carried her. This burden attached itself to me, like the baby butterfly on the brooch my friend had given me. It was an unhealthy state altogether. I was burdened and burnt-out; I confessed with my mouth that I belonged to God but my heart was far away from Him. I was saying that I am God's child, yet I lived like an orphan. I was proclaiming His love over me, yet I was desperately lonely. I was not doing the will of my Father in heaven, meaning I practiced lawlessness. This is what Jesus says about people practicing lawlessness:

> "Not everyone who says to Me, 'Lord, Lord', shall enter the kingdom of heaven, but he who does the will of My Father in heaven.
>
> Many will say to Me in that day, 'Lord, Lord, have we not prophesied in Your name, cast out demons in Your name, and done many wonders in Your name?'
>
> And then I will declare to them, 'I never knew you, depart from Me, you who practice lawlessness.'"
>
> (Matthew 7:21-23, NKJ)

How many of us have known or unknown secret foreskins around our hearts? Money can be a foreskin. What about depression, hurt, sensitivity, emotional complexes, anger, bitterness, unforgiveness, self-pity, jealousy, and other feelings? What prevents the God of our deliverance from touching us?

We read in the Bible we should work out our own salvation:

> "Therefore, my beloved, as you have always obeyed, not as in my presence only, but now much more in my absence, work out your own salvation with fear and trembling;
>
> for it is God who works in you both to will and to do for His good pleasure." (Philippians 2:12-13, NKJ)

If we should work out our own salvation, surely it means that we have to find the issues in our hearts that are preventing us from having an intimate relationship with God. Once we have identified those issues, we should burn, destroy or do away with them for good.

We read in Isaiah about the promise of the good news of salvation:

> "The Spirit of the Lord God is upon Me, because the Lord has anointed Me to preach good tidings to the poor; He has sent Me to heal the brokenhearted, to proclaim liberty to the captives, and the opening of the prison to those who are bound;
>
> To proclaim the acceptable year of the Lord, and the day of vengeance of our God; to comfort all who mourn.
>
> To console those who mourn in Zion, to give them beauty for ashes, the oil of joy for mourning, the garment of praise for the spirit of heaviness; that they may be called trees of righteousness, the planting of the Lord, that He may be glorified."
>
> (Isaiah 61:1-3, NKJ)

After Jesus had spent 40 days in the desert, He returned in the power of the Spirit, proclaiming that the promise of salvation had been fulfilled by quoting Isaiah 61 in Luke 4:18-19.

Who needs healing; to be set free; to see or to be comforted? Who needs beauty, oil of joy and a garment of praise? We all do. We all need to work out our own salvation so that we can receive the promises of God.

At this point I realized I was halfway up the mountain. I chose the route of submitting to God and the rest of the climb seemed so easy. God was doing everything. The footpath curled around a bend, bringing me to a standstill. I could not believe my eyes. The second route that I chose not to take merged into the one I was on. The footpath narrowed, a dark cloud hung over the mountain and thorns and thistles appeared on the trees. I heard roaring like that of a lion, with dangerous snakes lurking in the trees. A wicked laughter brought me to my knees.

It felt unfair. My struggle was between God and me. How dare a third person intervene! Who gave him the right to be there? I knew why he was there. He was going to scare me off this mountain. I was coming too close to God and the devil did not like it.

According to Matthew 4:1-11, the devil tempted Jesus in three aspects when He spent forty days in the wilderness. Jesus had not eaten for forty days and the devil tempted Him with bread. The devil promised that he could satisfy the hunger pains of Jesus. In my climb up the mountain, I became tired. I was tempted to fill myself on resting, sleeping and reading. In my circle of friends and acquaintances I knew of no one who had reached the Promised Land. They were all struggling on their way. My worldly friends looked relaxed and happy. It was a choice between the meat of Egypt or the journey that leads to the milk and honey of the Promised Land. Some days the top of the mountain became blurred but the bottom always looked lush and green. I often wanted to give up.

One day Charl and I went climbing a steep hill in Christchurch. At one stage I became physically too tired to carry on. I sat down, refusing to go further. Charl kept urging me on, saying that although we could not see the top we were very close to it. For his sake, I made one last attempt to carry on, to find it was true - we reached the top of the hill!

For my own sake I could easily say yes to the devil and return to a lifestyle of reading, sleeping and playing. Somehow in the climb up Mount Horeb, I felt I did not do it for my sake only. Maybe this is what made Jesus turn the devil's offer down. For His own sake, He could fill His hunger on bread. But Jesus had come to take all of us who believe in Him to spend eternity with our Father. If He submitted to the devil then all of us would go down with Him. I did not know for whom else I was climbing up Mount Horeb. Maybe it was for the sake of my family, or friends and acquaintances, or for someone I did not know, maybe for you reading this book. It felt as if the angels were urging me on, as if the prayers of Jesus were enticing me to go higher. I knew from Revelation 8:4 that all the past and present prayers ascended to God. I knew I was not alone, and if I succumbed to the devil's offer, all those for whom I was climbing would go down with me. For their sake, I could not give up.

In the second temptation the devil dares Jesus to find out how much He means to God. Jesus refuses by replying that you cannot tempt God.

Often in my walk with God I looked at someone and thought God loved that person more than me, or the reason why God did not answer my prayers was because I was not one of His favourites. It is tempting to find out how much we mean to God. Will He save us if we do something dangerous? I wanted God to answer my prayers. When God did not respond, I seriously questioned my worth. The devil kept accusing me, bringing me down. I was tempted to give God an ultimatum, something like, 'If you love Resje, you would heal her'. It was very difficult for me to believe that He loved us, yet said no to our requests. I found it emotionally draining every time God said no to a request of mine. By rejecting my requests, I thought He was rejecting me. I had to fight the desire to stop asking God for anything and stop communicating with Him altogether. The devil plagued me with thoughts like, 'He is never going to help you; you are not worthy of His time and effort; He does not care for you'.

In the Garden of Gethsemane Jesus prayed:

> "O My Father, if it is possible, let this cup pass from Me; nevertheless, not as I will, but as You will."
>
> (Matthew 26:39, NKJ)

Jesus knew God could do anything. He could work out another plan to save mankind. He was an obedient Son of

God, He walked in God's ways, He was without sin; He was filled with the Holy Spirit; He was God's beloved Son in whom Father God was well pleased. God did not love Jesus less when He said no to His Son's requests. In fact He was more pleased with Jesus when Jesus obeyed Him, sacrificing His own will:

> "…Behold, to obey is better than sacrifice."
>
> (1 Samuel 15:22b, NKJ)

I had to make the shift in my mind from thinking that God was ignoring me, to obey Him when He said 'no'. The devil wanted me to think lowly of myself. I had to walk past the roaring lion waiting to devour me:

> "Therefore humble yourselves under the mighty hand of God, that He may exalt you in due time,
>
> casting all your care upon Him, for He cares for you.
>
> Be sober, be vigilant; because your adversary the devil walks about like a roaring lion, seeking whom he may devour.
>
> Resist him, steadfast in the faith, knowing that the same sufferings are experienced by your brotherhood in the world." (1 Peter 5:6-9, NKJ)

The secret was in humility. If God said 'yes' to my prayer requests, I would have felt superior, special and chosen. The devil wanted me to think that I was a nuisance and an outcast if God did not answer my prayers positively. This meant that if I wanted God to show me that He loved and cared for me, then I had to test Him to see if He would say 'yes' to a request of mine.

To humble myself meant that I had to accept the 'no's' of God. I had to renew my mind to begin resisting the devil. This was a new and strange thought pattern that did not come naturally to me and it required that I put on the armour of God:

"Therefore take up the whole armor of God, that you may be able to withstand in the evil day, and having done all, to stand.

Stand therefore, having girded your waist with truth, having put on the breastplate of righteousness,

and having shod your feet with the preparation of the gospel of peace;

above all, taking the shield of faith with which you will be able to quench all the fiery darts of the wicked one.

And take the helmet of salvation, and the sword of the Spirit, which is the word of God;

praying always with all prayer and supplication in the Spirit, being watchful to this end with all perseverance and supplication for all the saints."

(Ephesians 6:13-18, NKJ)

Every time the devil, the roaring lion, stormed me I turned around and fled into a cave. There I would stay for days, weeks, before I had the strength to venture out again. I could not understand why God could not chase the roaring lion away. When I realized that God also did not chase the roaring lion away from His weak hungry Son after spending 40 days in the wilderness, I accepted that this was a hurdle Father God wanted me to overcome. With my armour on I had to go and learn from Jesus.

He resisted the devil, He had answers for him, He did not go into hiding and He did not accept what the devil was telling Him.

The change came through Resje. For myself I was weak, but for my little girl I always had to be strong or pretend that I was.

A roaring lion lashed out at Resje one day, scaring her so that she fled into a cave. I ran with her, but because he was attacking my daughter I turned around. I saw his cruel, aggressive eyes. Hatred and death were in them. He snarled at me for turning around and then I saw it. He had no teeth. The roaring lion was towering over a Slain Lamb pretending that he had killed it; I lifted my head and saw the Good Shepherd with a bag containing the lion's teeth. He pulled them out one by one on a hill in Calvary long ago. The Good Shepherd was waiting for us to join the other sheep in His paddock. We had to get out of the cave. He was not even asking us to walk past the lion; He knew the lion would crawl back to where he had come from. I got up from my crouching position and called to Resje.

Every time someone tries to belittle you, you can hear the roaring lion. He succeeds in scaring you the moment you think you are unworthy, not important in the eyes of God, an outcast, a lost sinner, a failure. We then want to fight him back on the grounds of humanity with proud thoughts of, 'we are not that bad, we all need a place in the sun, look at our achievements, we are important, there is something good in each of us'. Because of this attitude we find it difficult to humble ourselves to enter the Kingdom of God. We confuse humility with unworthiness. The Bible says we should stand, not fight him. To stand means we do not accept what he says, we do not run away and we do not hide. It is not what we think about ourselves that is important. I have found that my thinking has brought me nowhere. Humbly we must accept what God says about us. And He says the following:

> "Are not two sparrows sold for a copper coin? And not one of them falls to the ground apart from your Father's will.
>
> But the very hairs of your head are all numbered.
>
> Do not fear therefore; you are of more value than many sparrows." (Matthew 10:29-31, NKJ);

> "Fear not, for I have redeemed you; I have called you by your name; you are Mine.

> When you pass through the waters, I will be with you; and through the rivers, they shall not overflow you. When you walk through the fire, you shall not be burned. Nor shall the flame scorch you.
>
> For I am the Lord your God, the Holy One of Israel, your Savior". (Isaiah 43:1b-3, NKJ)

I stood, facing the toothless roaring lion. I had been hurt enough. My daughter had been hurt enough. It was time for God who lives in us to arise. What He says is all-powerful, true and everlasting. He did not have to heal my daughter to show me His love. I do not have to test Him on this. I have found out for myself and now know He loves me.

The lion crept back into the darkness of the cloud that surrounded the mountain. A streak of sunlight came through before it turned dark again.

The third request the devil asked of Jesus was that He turn His back on God and worship him instead.

It was a final attempt - to receive from the devil whatever my heart desired if I only turned my back on God. My heart's desire was for Resje's health. It was a choice between Resje's healing and God, a circumcision of my heart or a turning away.

Of course you can have both. In my case her healing stood between God and me. I had my priorities wrong. I wanted to find God through Resje's healing. God wanted me to find Him for His sake. I had to give up on her healing, to seek "first the Kingdom of God and His righteousness".

I gave the devil one look. I had come too far to turn around. Jesus spent 40 days in the wilderness. I was there for nearly twenty years. I will never believe that Resje's suffering, which my eyes have seen, and her groans, which my ears have heard were by chance, or for nothing, or some unique case in a million. It happened for a reason, a purpose. God was the reason and the purpose. I found Him. I was not going to let go of Him. He was waiting for me in the Promised Land.

Slowly, I let go of my desire. I turned my back on the devil. I chose to worship God, my Heavenly Father.

I looked up to find that I had reached the top of Mount Horeb. God could not come down from His cloud because of the foreskin still around my heart. I was unholy, He was the only One who could help me, I cried out to Him:

Father God, I no longer want anything to stand between You and me. I want to give You my heart. I do not want Resje or anything else to come between us. Help me.

I looked up to the cloud. Clearly, I could see God as if in a hospital theatre, preparing for the circumcision. He was holding a scalpel in His hand. He came a few steps closer and then stopped. I realized He was going to do it. He was going to cut away the foreskin. The operating table was ready. I looked over my shoulder once more at Resje. She was sleeping. Her long hair spread over the pillow. I was glad for this moment of peace on her beautiful face. I knew she would soon awake and start scratching, her face wrought with irritation.

"Resh," I whispered, *"Many daughters have done well, but you excel them all."* (Proverbs 31:29, NKJ)

She did not move.

"I am letting you go, my girl. You are free to fly into your Father's loving arms. His arms are stronger, His love purer and His faithfulness is greater than mine. He surrounds you with His presence. He is your

Almighty King, your Maker and your Husband. He is waiting for you to keep you and bless you, to heal and restore, to forgive and to love, to wipe away your tears and to make all things new. You are His Talitha. He is calling out to you: 'Talitha, cumi'. He wants to give you life for evermore. Go, my darling Resh, go to Him, go."

I put on my white theatre gown, noticing there was no anaesthetist. I lay down on the operating table and closed my eyes to hear music. It was coming from somewhere above. With strained ears, I tried to identify the staccato notes, realizing in this intimate moment the sound from heaven I was waiting for was not the wind - it was music! The music brought a third person into the room. I instinctively knew He was the Holy Spirit.

God bent over to touch me. I felt His hand of ownership on my heart. It was the hand of my Bridegroom, my Maker and my Husband. I gave myself over to the anaesthesia of the music. I heard it, loud and clear. It was the Wedding March, triumphantly reverberating in my ears and heart.

Chapter Eight

THE HIGHWAY OF HOLINESS

"Behold, your God will come with vengeance, with the recompense of God; He will come and save you.

Then the eyes of the blind shall be opened, and the ears of the deaf shall be unstopped.

Then the lame shall leap like a deer, and the tongue of the dumb sing. For waters shall burst forth in the wilderness, and streams in the desert."

(Isaiah 35:4b – 6, NKJ)

"A highway shall be there, and a road, and it shall be called the Highway of Holiness. The unclean shall not pass over it, but it shall be for others. Whoever walks the road, although a fool, shall not go astray.

No lion shall be there, nor shall any ravenous beast go up on it; it shall not be found there. But the redeemed shall walk there,

And the ransomed of the Lord shall return, and come to Zion with singing, with everlasting joy on their heads. They shall obtain joy and gladness, and sorrow and sighing shall flee away." (Isaiah 35:8-10, NKJ)

I knew what God was saying to me. The Highway of Holiness had been there all along. I could have gone on it a long time ago, if only I had realized it. The journey of my life had not been in vain; the journey up my few mountains had made me strong and fit, aware of the Highway. The fog sharpened my eyesight and the stillness my hearing. One day I looked past the fog, heard past the quiet, and there it was: the Highway of Holiness. I looked up the steep hill to the top. The mountain was called Mount Zion and God's palace was built at the very top.

I had arrived, but not at the top; it was still a long climb. Something within warned me the climb would take the rest of my earthly days, but I had reached Mount Zion, the dwelling place of the Almighty God.

> "But you have come to Mount Zion and to the city of the living God, the heavenly Jerusalem, to an innumerable company of angels."
>
> (Hebrews 12:22, NKJ)

I fell prostrate before the Lord.

Why am I here, Father God?

He answered me:

> "But on Mount Zion there shall be deliverance, and there shall be holiness…" (Obadiah 1:17, NKJ)

What am I doing on this holy mountain?

> "Walk about Zion, and go all around her. Count her towers;
>
> Mark well her bulwarks; consider her palaces; that you may tell it to the generation following.

> For this is God, our God forever and ever; He will be our guide even to death." (Psalm 48:12-14, NKJ)

What will happen here, Lord?

> "Now it shall come to pass in the latter days that the mountain of the Lord's house shall be established on the top of the mountains, and shall be exalted above the hills; and peoples shall flow to it.
>
> Many nations shall come and say, 'Come and let us go up to the mountain of the Lord, to the house of the God of Jacob; He will teach us His ways, and we shall walk in His paths.' For out of Zion the law shall go forth, and the word of the Lord from Jerusalem." (Micah 4:1-2, NKJ)

> "'In that day,' says the Lord, 'I will assemble the lame, I will gather the outcast and those whom I have afflicted;
>
> I will make the lame a remnant, and the outcast a strong nation;' so the Lord will reign over them in Mount Zion from now on, even forever."
>
> (Micah 4:6-7, NKJ)

I took off my shoes. Instinctively I knew this Highway was a holy road. The Holiness spread from the top down to the beginning of the path. His Holy Spirit was waiting for me to commence the journey. He was holding out His Hand. This time I would not depend on my reasoning abilities, talents or emotions. The Holy Spirit would be my guide to lead me to the top. He would teach me the ways of God and He would hold my hand firm in His to help me to walk in His paths. In the past I had always wanted to conquer a journey in my own might and power. Humbly, I turned to take the Hand of the Holy Spirit. It is by His Spirit that I will enjoy victory.

I looked up. Who am I to come closer to Holiness? I'd blamed God, turned my anger, hatred and back on Him. I'd fought Him, accusing Him of rejecting me. Then I served Him for my sake, wanting Him to heal Resje. I was false, a deceiver and a conniver. Now a loving and forgiving Father was sending me His Spirit to help me to come closer to Him. I was blind and deaf, lame and mute. Who am I that He should choose me? I was not worthy to venture near this mountain.

> "And I heard a loud voice from heaven saying, 'Behold, the tabernacle of God is with men, and He will dwell with them, and they shall be His people. God Himself will be with them and be their God.
>
> And God will wipe away every tear from their eyes; there shall be no more death, nor sorrow, nor crying. There shall be no more pain, for the former things have passed away.'
>
> Then He who sat on the throne said, 'Behold, I make all things new.' And He said to me, 'Write, for these words are true and faithful.'
>
> And He said to me, 'It is done! I am the Alpha and the Omega, the Beginning and the End. I will give of the fountain of the water of life freely to him who thirsts.
>
> He who overcomes shall inherit all things, and I will be his God and he shall be My son.'"
>
> (Revelation 21:3-7, NKJ)

My flesh was rotten and sinful. I was bad. But I was thirsty, not primarily for Him but for the things of His Kingdom: joy, peace, health and everlasting life. And He bent down and chose me for His bride. I will never be able to comprehend His ways, His grace and His love.

The Highway stretched out. There was something familiar about it, as if someone had previously described it to me, yet I hesitated to start the journey. It was holy ground and I feared the Holiness.

One of the seven angels in Revelation said to John:

> "Come, I will show you the bride, the Lamb's wife." (Revelation 21:9b, NKJ)

I thought of a beautiful woman, dressed in white with a perfect outward appearance. This is the angel's description:

> "And he carried me away in the Spirit to a great and high mountain, and showed me the great city, the holy Jerusalem, descending out of heaven from God, having the glory of God. Her light was like a most precious stone, like a jasper stone, clear as crystal.
>
> Also she had a great and high wall with twelve gates, and twelve angels at the gates, and names written on them, which are the names of the twelve tribes of the children of Israel: three gates on the east, three gates on the north, three gates on the south, and three gates on the west.
>
> Now the wall of the city had twelve foundations, and on them were the names of the twelve apostles of the Lamb." (Revelation 21:10-14, NKJ)

> "The construction of its wall was of jasper; and the city was pure gold, like clear glass.
>
> The foundations of the wall of the city were adorned with all kinds of precious stones: the first foundation was jasper, the second sapphire, the third chalcedony, the fourth emerald,
>
> the fifth sardonyx, the sixth sardius, the seventh chrysolite, the eighth beryl, the ninth topaz, the tenth chrysoprase, the eleventh jacinth, and the twelfth amethyst.

The twelve gates were twelve pearls: each individual gate was of one pearl. And the street of the city was pure gold, like transparent glass."

(Revelation 21:18-21, NKJ)

Father God was not looking at our flesh. Whether we had two legs, one leg or none; physical eyes and ears or not; pretty or ugly faces; a perfect skin or one covered in tumours. He did not use our outward appearances but our circumcised hearts to build a bride for His Son. My heart began to beat loudly. I felt so unworthy. I could not even circumcise my own heart - Father God had to do it. Something within me caused excitement to bubble up.

In front of the entrance to the Holy Palace, I saw a secret passage to a garden. It was the Garden of Eden - Paradise. That was our original dwelling place where we were meant to live forever without pain and death, in the presence of Holiness, but because of Adam and Eve's sin, the Garden gates were closed. God was holy, only holy people could enter into His presence.

I looked at the Highway leading to God. Suddenly I understood the mystery of Christianity. I had the keys to unlock the Heavenlies. I had found the secret. The veil in front of my face fell off, my blind eyes saw, my deaf ears heard the angels singing and my lame feet started dancing. Like David dancing in front of the tabernacle, I did the same. I danced for Him, my Husband and my Maker. I knew God was smiling. He was holding out His handkerchief. This time, I would not turn my face from Him to wipe away my tears. Inexpressible joy filled my soul.

When God created Adam and Eve, He did not want to create robots, compelling them to serve and obey Him. He created them free, without chains, desiring them to choose a life with Him out of their own free will, the free will that He gave them.

They did not choose Him for they could not resist the temptation.

God's laws forbade the unholy sinners to stay in His Garden. For centuries He tried everything to lure them back to the Highway. He became angry, He threatened, punished and begged. Only the sacrificial blood of an animal could pay for their sins. The Highway leading to Him had permanent red stains from the spilt blood of the sacrificial animals throughout the ages. In the entire world, there was not one human holy enough to stand in His presence. God had to come forth with yet another solution.

Two thousand years ago Father God sent His own heart, His Son Jesus Christ, into the world. He had two duties to perform. He had to show people the heart of God and He had to pay for their sins. God's heart was filled with love and compassion. He wanted to heal, restore, protect and save mankind from utter destruction. Miracle upon miracle took place. When the wine at the wedding ran out, Jesus made more. He healed the lepers, He opened blind eyes, healed the deaf, mute and lame. He cast out demons, freeing, blessing, loving and forgiving people. This was the heart of Father God. God did all of this in the hope that if He showed us His heart, one day we would change our hearts too. We would love Him in return as He loves us; receive Him as the bridegroom in the same way He wants us for His bride.

Strangely enough, that was not what the people wanted. By now sin and Satan had numbed our minds. We rejected the love and mercy, the forgiveness and the healing of a heavenly Creator. We hated and despised His heart. We stripped, whipped and crucified Jesus. For the last time God would need one final sacrifice on the Highway to Him: His Son's blood, His own blood. This Highway would be the road of His Son's suffering where the world openly rejected and killed the God of the Universe.

Then Father God did a strange and unusual thing, the unthinkable. He decided to turn this same road of suffering and rejection into a sacred and holy road. His tears of pain, rejection and hurt filled the Highway, washing off the blood of the many animal sacrifices throughout the centuries.

He then laid the sin of the whole world on the road. God was at the top of Mount Zion; we were at the bottom. Between us was a road filled with sin, separating and distancing us from God. With His Son's blood He smeared the Highway, covering our sins, turning the filthy highway into Holy Ground.

The blood of one human being was enough to wash away the past, present and future sin of the world, because this one human being was not only the Son of Man; He was also the Son of God. One drop of God's holy blood was enough to pay for the sins of His children.

We are all literally and figuratively the children of Adam, the children of God:

> "And He has made from one blood every nation of men to dwell on all the face of the earth, and has determined their preappointed times and the boundaries of their dwellings." (Acts 17:26, NKJ)

This was the reason why the Highway was familiar to me. I had read about it repeatedly in the Bible. I had heard about it since I was a baby. It is the message of Christianity, the hope that lies in Christ Jesus. Jesus Christ is the Highway to Holiness. Jesus, the Son of God, had done it all for us. His Holy blood makes it possible to enter into God's presence:

> "And His name will be called Wonderful, Counselor, Mighty God, Everlasting Father, Prince of Peace."
>
> (Isaiah 9:6b, NKJ);

> "Worthy is the Lamb who was slain to receive power and riches and wisdom, and strength and honor and glory and blessing!" (Revelation 5:12, NKJ);

> "Blessing and honor and glory and power be to Him who sits on the throne, and to the Lamb, forever and ever!" (Revelation 5:13b, NKJ).

The exact unthinkable transformation that Father God has done with the Highway, He is doing with us. He is turning the same filthy hearts filled with sin and hatred into hearts of pure gold and precious jewels.

If Jesus has done it all for us, transforming the Highway into a holy place and Father God circumcises our hearts, then what do we have to do? I went from striving in my own strength to reach God to the opposite of doing nothing until I finally reached God's answer.

We cannot go up Mount Zion to God except through Jesus Christ. Jesus said:

> "I am the door. If anyone enters by Me, he will be saved, and will go in and out and find pasture."
>
> (John 10:9, NKJ)

To begin the climb up the mountain we do it in the name and character of Jesus Christ, adapting to His nature. First we have to be found worthy enough to follow Him:

> "He who loves father or mother more than Me is not worthy of Me. And he who loves son or daughter more than Me is not worthy of Me.
>
> And he who does not take his cross and follow after Me is not worthy of Me." (Matthew 10:37-39, NKJ)

I was found not worthy because I loved myself more than my Creator. The God of the Universe had to teach me about love through suffering. Then I was still not found worthy because I loved Resje more than Him but slowly with much patience, grace and love He remained standing until He opened my eyes and ears. He unlocked and circumcised my heart and I let Him in to take His rightful place in the centre of my heart. I was still making many mistakes, more than I could count, but my heart wanted to follow Him.

> "If anyone desires to come after Me, let him deny himself, and take up his cross, and follow Me.
>
> For whoever desires to save his life will lose it, but whoever loses his life for My sake will find it."
>
> (Matthew 16:24-25, NKJ)

Although Jesus has done it all for us, repairing and restoring the broken relationship between man and God and giving us the right to eat of the fruit of eternal life, there is a prerequisite. We cannot simply wait at the bottom of the mountain for the angels to carry us across the Highway to the bosom of Father God. Would that not be wonderful! We have to pick up our crosses and die to everything that is of the flesh while walking the Highway following Jesus:

> "For if you live according to the flesh you will die; but if by the Spirit you put to death the deeds of the body, you will live." (Romans 8:13, NKJ)

We have the example of the Son of Man and how He walked on earth. Because He and His Father were one, His Father was in Him and He in His Father, He walked in victory. He is the Son of God and filled with the Holy Spirit to perform miracles, to cast out demons, to raise the dead. So we can be conquerors in our climb up Mount Zion. We are children of ordinary, sinful men and women, but we have the Spirit of the Almighty God living in us, and we in Him:

> "At that day you will know that I am in My Father, and you in Me, and I in you." (John 14:20, NKJ)

Being His children makes it possible for us to willingly and victoriously lay down our flesh. It is not easy to carry our cross, to set it up and crucify our flesh with its passions and desires daily, but it is possible by the power of the Holy Spirit.

On the journey up Mount Zion we have to follow in the footsteps of Jesus, becoming like Him. When we show people the heart of God we show them compassion, kindness, gentleness and love. We embrace the needy, care for the sick, the widows and orphans. To become like Jesus means we have to deny ourselves many things, die to our fleshly passions and desires, humble ourselves, walk in forgiveness and be obedient to Father God. Praise be to God that He knew we would never be able to do this in our own strength. He had to send us His Holy Spirit to help, teach and remind us, to fill us with Godly strength to stand against the evil one, to keep the faith and to remain true to our calling.

The Highway was beckoning me to begin the journey. I had the Holy Spirit as my companion. Like Lot's wife, fortunately without turning into stone, I looked back for the last time. For a brief moment there was a fleshly yearning to the state I was in twenty years ago, worshiping myself, feeling good and happy in my perfect worldly existence. Praise God who dramatically interfered and interrupted my life.

He gave me Resje.

She filled my world with her pain and agony, her suffering and hurt. It took me on a journey where I found the Creator of Life where I asked Him where He was when we needed Him. He answered me with a question: 'Where were you when I wanted you?' His rejection filled my soul. His pain and hurt, suffering and blood flooded my spirit.

Unlike the persecutor of the Christian Church, Saul of Tarsus, who turned virtually overnight into Paul, a devoted follower of Jesus, I gradually began to know the true God of love and mercy, walking closer to Him. Paul's blind eyes were opened within three days. It took the Living God nearly twenty years of patiently stroking mine before I could also see the Lord of lords, the King of kings, the Almighty Saviour, the Alpha and the Omega, the Creator of the Universe, the great I AM. He never gave up on me and He never stopped loving me.

I turned, facing Mount Zion. I thought I heard God whispering to me, asking me if I wanted to turn back. There was hesitation in His voice but no anger or reproach. I answered Him the same words as Peter:

> "Lord, to whom shall (I) go? You have the words of eternal life.
>
> Also (I) have come to believe and know that You are the Christ, the Son of the living God."
>
> (John 6:68-69, NKJ).

I knew I could never ascend in my own strength. But I was wondering what was waiting for me. How should I die to my flesh? What fleshly nature should I need to crucify? My burdens did not constitute the cross that I needed to pick up and carry. I was required to lay them down at the foot of Jesus. I reasoned with God, finding out from Him what was required. It was different to my past where I had wanted to find God with my intellect. I knew now that God was speaking to my heart and that I had to be obedient to Him. But He gave me my mind to also explore and reason with Him. The answer was found in Matthew:

> "When the Son of Man comes in His glory, and all the holy angels with Him, then He will sit on the throne of His glory.

All the nations will be gathered before Him, and He will separate them one from another, as a shepherd divides his sheep from the goats.

And He will set the sheep on His right hand, but the goats on the left.

Then the King will say to those on His right hand, 'Come, you blessed of My Father, inherit the kingdom prepared for you from the foundation of the world:

For I was hungry and you gave Me food; I was thirsty and you gave Me drink; I was a stranger and you took Me in;

I was naked and you clothed Me; I was sick and you visited Me; I was in prison and you came to Me.'

Then the righteous will answer Him, saying, 'Lord, when did we see You hungry and feed You, or thirsty and give You drink?

When did we see You a stranger and take You in, or naked and clothe You?

Or when did we see You sick, or in prison, and come to You?'

And the King will answer and say to them, 'Assuredly, I say to you, inasmuch as you did it to one of the least of these My brethren, you did it to Me.'"

(Matthew 25:31-40, NKJ)

With Peter's restoration Jesus asked him to feed and tend His sheep and lambs. Now He was asking me to lay down my flesh for my fellowmen. This was the very last hurdle for me to cross before I could continue my journey. I felt empty and poor, naked and thirsty, sick and hungry, poor and lonely, an outcast in a strange land. How could I give if I did not have anything? I was one of the sheep of Jesus who needed feeding and tending.

God spoke to me:

> "So He humbled you, allowed you to hunger, and fed you with manna which you did not know nor did your fathers know, that He might make you know that man shall not live by bread alone; but man lives by every word that proceeds from the mouth of the Lord."
>
> (Deuteronomy 8:3, NKJ)

Yes, Lord all other things are secondary to You. You alone give life. But what do I give to people who are hungry?

> "…man lives by every word that proceeds from the mouth of the Lord." (Deuteronomy 8:3b, NKJ)

Do you want me to give them Your words? How do I do that?

> "You shall receive power when the Holy Spirit has come upon you; and you shall be witnesses to Me in Jerusalem, and in all Judea and Samaria, and to the end of the earth." (Acts 1:8, NKJ)

This is all you want me to do? Do You want me to be a witness for You wherever I go, speak the words of Jesus and display the character of Jesus to others? I can never be like Jesus. That is exactly what I have been trying to tell You. How can I heal the sick, feed the hungry, clothe the naked if I am sick, hungry and naked?

> "For the Lord your God is bringing you into a good land, a land of brooks of water, of fountains and springs, that flow out of valleys and hills;
>
> a land of wheat and barley, of vines and fig trees and pomegranates, a land of olive oil and honey;

> a land in which you will eat bread without scarcity, in which you will lack nothing; a land whose stones are iron and out of whose hills you can dig copper.
>
> When you have eaten and are full, then you shall bless the lord your God for the good land which He has given you." (Deuteronomy 8:7-10, NKJ)

It felt like I was missing the point. I knew I had to crucify the flesh, not my soul. It was in my soul where I was hungry and naked and in need of healing and restoration. If I understood God correctly He would satisfy my hunger, clothe my nakedness and heal me, then I would be able to bless Him and share His blessings with others. I wondered when He would bring me into this land, and what was the cross of my flesh that I had to pick up and carry with me? The cross was the desires to feed and satisfy my flesh. What did my flesh want?

The same revelation that struck me when I realized that Jesus is the Highway to Holiness, struck me when I pondered on the words of Jesus in Luke when He read from the scriptures. Jesus quoted Isaiah 61:1-2 saying that the Spirit of the Lord God was upon Him to preach the good news, to heal and to set free. When He closed the book He said:

> "Today this Scripture is fulfilled in your hearing."
>
> (Luke 4:21, NKJ)

The reason why the Scripture was fulfilled that day was because Jesus was in their midst. The land that I was waiting to be led into was the Land of Jesus. Jesus is the Land of milk and honey. He is the bread, the olive oil and honey. Jesus is the Land of brooks and fountains, the Land of wheat and barley, of vines and fig trees and pomegranates. In Jesus I would lack nothing, my healing and restoration in Him would be complete. I had to cross the Jordan River to find Jesus. He is the Highway to Holiness. He is the way to the Father. He has given us salvation and everlasting life. He has done everything for us.

My duty was to eat from Him until I was full so that I could bless God for the good land that He had given me and share this blessing with others. To eat from Him meant to eat the bread of His body and drink His blood. That means we partake of Jesus and His suffering, letting Him enter our soul, mind and spirit. Once we do that He is in us as we are in Him, we become like Him because we are one. Our flesh can never receive Him because of the sin and lust in our flesh. We can never purify or cleanse our flesh. It needs to be put to death.

The desires of my flesh became clear to me. My flesh did not desire to be like Jesus. Jesus was a character strange and unwanted to my flesh. My flesh did not want to put other people first; it did not desire to look at the needs of other people. My flesh did not want to be like Jesus at all. On the contrary my flesh desired the opposite of the character of Jesus. That was my cross. My cross was everything that was not of Jesus. To be like Him meant to crucify my flesh. When we crucify our flesh, we show others what Jesus Christ did for us who believe in Him.

Jesus was sent by His Father to come to earth. From the earth He was sent to the grave. From the grave He was raised and lifted up to the Heavens. The same applies to us. Our Heavenly Father desires and conceives us in His heart, sends us specific circumstances in a specific place and time here on earth and fills us with His Holy Spirit so that we can show people His heart and crucify our flesh. When we do this we can walk as resurrected children of the living God. One day He will raise us up as His bride adorned with precious jewels and gems for us to live eternally at His side.

Barefooted, I started the journey. Like Miriam with her tambourine I danced and leapt with joy. My God had done all this for me. He had taken me out of the miry clay and put my feet upon a Rock. He had brought me to Mount Zion. He had prepared me for Him and made me worthy to ascend. He had made the Highway holy and flattened the stones. He had redeemed me and delivered me. He had kept me in the palm of His mighty Hand. He had loved me and fought for me. He is the Almighty God of the Universe, the Creator of the ends of the earth. He is the great I AM, my everlasting God.

You are the Lord of lords and holy. You are the Alpha and the Omega. You were and You are and You are to come. Your glorious Name is to be praised. Your sacrificial love is to be taken. Your great and marvelous works are to be blessed. Holy, holy, holy are You Lord God, the worthy Lamb, the mighty Lion. You are great and mighty. Blessing and honour and glory and power to You, my everlasting King.

Jesus loved to tell stories. So do I. I have shared with you the journey of my life, now I would like to share with you the story of my life:

There once was a Master who lived in a beautiful thick forest. Although everything in the forest belonged to him, he had to abide by the rules of the forest. He was lonely and yearned for a wife. He had magical powers and one day decided to make himself a wife. He fashioned the most beautiful baby girl. According to the rules of the forest he could not keep her for himself. She had to grow up and if she decided to return, he could marry her. He had to let go of her. Searching through his strong binoculars, he found her the best home in the whole world to grow up. The night before he delivered her, he could not sleep. He held the tiny baby in his arms and this is what he told her.

"My precious one, I am letting you go tomorrow for one reason only, and that is for you to grow up and to come back to me. I love and adore you; I have made you; you belong to me; you are my heart's desire, lovely and beautiful. The rules of the forest are strict. I cannot come to fetch you. I am only allowed to whisper to you, so you will have to listen carefully as you will not see me."

He pressed her against his chest so that she could hear his heartbeat. With his head against her face he prayed that she would not forget his smell. He hugged her tenderly, hoping she would feel him for evermore. One of his teardrops fell onto her lips. Gently he wiped it, praying that she would always remember the taste.

"I am sending you into a dangerous zone. The big bad wolf will try everything he can to prevent you from coming back to me. He is jealous of me and wants you for himself, but if you remember me I will keep him from hurting you. The forest will grow thicker, but if you remember me I will cut away the thorny bushes. There remains one more dangerous thing. I will have to operate on you tonight to insert a very important valve in your heart. It is called the valve of choice and it will stay open. You must guard this with all your heart, my little one. I cannot force you to come back to me. One day it will be your choice alone. Here comes the difficult part, my dearest one. The day you choose me the valve will close and your heart will stop beating. When you die, I will be there, you will hear my whisper, this is what I will say to you: 'Talitha, cumi!' If you respond to my whisper, the forest with its wolf and thick bushes will not be a hurting place anymore. I will raise you up, this will be the time to get ready for our wedding."

He gently rocked her. "Do not forget me, my little one. Remember me. Come back to me. I will always love you."

The next morning with sobbing cries the Master of the Forest delivered her to the chosen couple. He stood at the window, staring at her through moist eyes, not wanting to leave her. The couple pulled the curtains and he knew it was time to go back. He immediately took out his binoculars and zoomed in onto the little girl. He was not going to let her out of his sight for one second.

He watched her grow up, practising the option valve. When she chose good things he smiled, relaxing. When she chose bad things, he cried with her, wishing he could remove the mess she had made. He often saw her smelling the air, licking her lips, smiling. When he whispered, he could see that she heard him. She could not see him, but she often came outside the house, staring at the forest. She was remembering him!

The years went by. She grew up into a beautiful woman. Then one day when he whispered her name, she did not look up. He sat up. This could not be. He noticed she had stopped licking her lips and smelling the air. Tears rolled down his face. He fell on his knees, beating his chest. He knew the harsh rules of the forest, praying he would never have to apply them. For days he whispered her name, refusing to give up. He put lovely flowers on the path to remind her to smell the air. She only looked at them and walked past. At long last he sat down. With loud cries, the Master of the Forest admitted to himself: she had forgotten him.

He fetched the book, staring in disbelief at the rules. How could he do this to her? She was soft and tender hearted. He had held her heart in his hands when he had put the option valve in. She was vulnerable and fragile. How would she ever survive alone in the forest? He clenched his jaw. There was nothing that he could do. He had to follow the rules. He looked at the book:

> Rule number 1: 'Stop cutting away the thorny bushes and thickets.'
>
> Rule number 2: 'Stop preventing the wolf from getting close.'
>
> Rule number 3…

He could not read anymore. Throwing the Rule Book under the table, he pulled the binoculars closer. The bush closed in on her quickly. He watched how the thorns were pulling flesh from her soft skin. He knew the poisonous thorns would leave permanent scars. He saw the grin on the wolf's face and turned his face away. Tears rolled down his cheeks. He did not want to see the pain and suffering which he could not stop. The valve in her heart was the only key that could stop the hurt. If only she would remember and choose him. He fell on his knees, praying.

"How long before you remember me, my darling one?"

He cried, prayed and whispered to her but to no avail. It was an ongoing battle between her survival and the dangers of the forest. Blood and puss were running from her open wounds. He longed to pour oil on them, clean them and kiss them better. The years came and went.

Then one glorious day she looked up, past the thickets and the bush, past the wolf and the forest. A teardrop fell on her cheek. Frowning, she tasted it, smelled the air. He whispered her name; she tilted her head. Faster and faster his heart beat.

"I will heal your wounds, we will invite everyone to our wedding, my precious one, we will laugh, sing and dance until we can no more. Remember me, my little one, remember me!"

She lay herself down on her bed, closed her eyes to the forest, the wolf, the life of pain and suffering and faintly heard a familiar voice whispering to her: "Talitha, cumi!"

Do you too, beloved reader, hear His whispers?

Do you too remember His smell, His taste, His Holiness?

Will you too choose Him?

Have you too felt His teardrops on your face?

Go lay yourself down my friend. Close your eyes to the world of pain and suffering. He is calling you. Go. Go to Him and live.

PART FOUR

ENTERING THE PROMISED LAND

Chapter Nine

MY HERITAGE, REWARD AND ARROWS
(Healing and restoration of my motherhood)

> "Behold, children are a heritage from the Lord, the fruit of the womb is a reward.
>
> Like arrows in the hand of a warrior, so are the children of one's youth."(Psalm 127, 3-4, NKJ)

> "And Adam was not deceived, but the woman being deceived, fell into transgression. Nevertheless she will be saved in childbearing if they continue in faith, love, and holiness, with self-control."
>
> (1 Timothy 2:14-15, NKJ)

Whilst still living in Zimbabwe, during one of my long trips to the University, God revealed to me that He wanted to heal me in all areas of my life. Just as He is the Trinity God, our identity is a complicated issue. The day I got married, I became a wife, a second person. The day Resje was born, I became a mother, a third person. Not only was His purpose to restore my womanhood; He also wanted to restore my motherhood and my identity as a wife. Healing and restoring all three aspects of my being would bring the fullness of God's healing touch.

Resje turned 26 on 31 August 2014. As a form of endearment, people who know her well, including her mother, call her Resh. In the Jerusalem Bible, the Classical alphabet is included in Proverbs 31. Each verse begins with a letter of the alphabet, "Aleph, Beth, Ghimel," and so on. The letter "Resh" is printed with Proverbs 31:29. It is as if God specially dedicated to her this verse:

> "*Resh* Many women have done admirable things, but you surpass them all".

The New King James Translation also says it beautifully:

> "Many daughters have done well, but you excel them all."

This verse says it all and what makes it so special is that it is as if God Himself affirms her with a word of encouragement.

When she was little I saw the naevi hiding her beautiful skin. After the procedures began, the scars hid my little girl and the irritation prevented her from enjoying life. Then I discovered Revelation 5 where John looks around to seek the Lion of Judah only to find the slain Lamb. One day I looked past the naevi, the scars and the scratching. I looked deeply into her eyes and went right into her soul. She was only disfigured on the outside. The elder looked with the eyes of his heart right into the Lamb's heart and saw Jesus had the heart of a lion. John looked with his physical eyes and saw the slain Lamb. That day, the eyes of my heart functioned and I could not find any black naevi, thick keloid scars or any itching and scratching in Resje's heart. Exactly like the elder in the Book of Revelation, I found the brave heart of a lioness.

I immediately understood what God said to Samuel when he had to find and anoint the young shepherd-boy, David, as God's chosen king of Israel:

> "Do not look at his appearance or at his physical stature, because I have refused him. For the Lord does not see as man sees; for man looks at the outward appearance, but the Lord looks at the heart."

(1 Samuel 16:7, NKJ)

In this chapter, I would love to share a little bit more of Resje and what the heart of a young lioness looks like. In observing her healthy heart, I discovered how God was restoring my motherhood.

She is a child of the living God, loving Him deeply. She walks closely with Him and hears His voice. She is humble and loving and does not look down on anyone. She is the most gracious person I have ever come across. She forgives seventy times seven with a smile on her face. Her career dreams and desires are to lessen the suffering of people. She is bright and bubbly with a wonderful sense of humour. She is tender and caring, emotional when she learns of other people's hurt.

Her face is beautiful. She has a crown of long, curly, black hair. Her tender eyes penetrate the depths of one's soul. A gorgeous smile that is nearly always on her lips lights up your world.

When she was eight months old, the plastic surgeon began operating on her legs. Her legs were put in plaster casts to prevent movement so that the stitches would not tear. During this period of nearly two years her legs were in casts for three weeks out of four, being free for one week prior to the next operation. I wondered how it was going to influence her walking. She crawled at eight months but further activity was hampered, limiting her movement. The week, however, that she had the casts taken off gave her the opportunity to explore the world. She realized she had less time than others to develop and had some catching up to do. She started walking at eleven months, an unbelievable sight. She made one determined effort to go forward and she went, as if she walked all her life.

Because the plaster casts did not prevent her from walking, it brought new problems to the surgeon. While she had the casts on, she developed a gait, swinging her stiff legs forward. After one specific operation, the doctor did not want her to be mobile at all. He totally covered her feet with the plaster casts, making the soles of the casts as round as tennis balls. That night, ten hours after the operation she got onto her round tennis ball plaster casts and walked without assistance. She was about eighteen months old. I phoned the surgeon immediately at his home. He laughingly, in an unbelieving voice, said it was impossible for her to walk. I asked him if he wanted to see it for himself, because while we were having this conversation on the phone, she was walking up and down on her round plaster casts. There was a long silence on the phone. His words were very clear: "If she can walk on those rounded soles, you should not stop her. Let her walk!"

The doctor realized what I had begun to notice about her. There were certain things that were more important to her than her operations. The operations were not going to stop her from living.

One day, at the age of three when Resje was trying to understand why people stared at her, she sat on a bench at the Zimbabwean/South African border. It was 40 degrees Celsius. She sat scratching herself. Both her knees were exposed. They were both covered with black naevi. A two-year old boy came up to her and pointed at her knees. She stopped scratching, bent down to the little boy and confided in him that she has a big "ouch" on her back too. Satisfied with this information the little boy wandered back to his parents. She has never turned away from someone genuinely interested in her.

At the age of four, I wondered how I could make her aware of the fact that there are many people who are in worse situations, without hurting her feelings. One day she said to me: "You know mom, this skin condition is not so bad. Look at how many people are blind and deaf. Look at how many people cannot walk." From that day on, I have noticed how she is burdened by someone else's suffering. She believes God made her strong to carry her own burden and also the burdens of others.

Resje started school in Zimbabwe at the age of five, in accordance with the Zimbabwean Education System. When she was too hot in the classroom to concentrate on her work, the teacher sent her to the hostel where she was put in a cold shower. Zimbabweans are used to a hot climate. The school that she attended had no air conditioning. She took a fan with her to school to cool off when she was too hot. At the beginning of each year the fan went with her to the next class. Operations were scheduled for the school holidays to minimize absenteeism during the term. She easily progressed to the next level each year. For two years from the age of seven, she wore pressure garments underneath her school uniform to lessen excessive scarring. The school would have granted her special permission to wear cooler clothing than the prescribed uniform, but she would not allow us to ask for special favours. She did not want to be different, but to look and be just like the other children. She attended two years of high school in Zimbabwe before we moved to New Zealand. The school and the friends she made in New Zealand opened their hearts for her and accepted her immediately as one of them and not as someone different.

Through the years, she continued to get up and walk as soon as possible after each operation. This was her Mount Everest to be conquered and nothing would stop her from doing so.

For nine years, her grandfather, my dad, accompanied us to the hospital with every operation. His death prevented him from fulfilling this duty to the end. When she became too heavy for me to carry her into the hospital, he carried her. He prayed with me while Resje was in the operating theatre, not only for his granddaughter, but also for the hospital staff and the plastic surgeon, whom he loved and respected. He cried with her when she awoke from the anaesthetic, in excruciating pain and agony. He helped me to bath her and to change her dressings. He sat with her while she was awake, then he sat with me when she fell asleep. Often he would silently stare at what the doctor had cut away and then wisely declare that it would not be possible for her to walk for a few days. Repeatedly, she would prove him wrong - no pain was going to prevent her from getting up.

My father together with our parents, grandmother, brothers and sisters, nephews and nieces, pastors and friends all supported us in the struggle to survive. They were always there, walking with us every step of the way, caring, encouraging, praying and interceding. Almost every person who came into contact with Resje became involved: neighbours, teachers, colleagues, doctors and medical staff - in South Africa, Zimbabwe and in New Zealand. She was on prayer lists all over the world. I know for sure that God will honour each and every one of the many people who were involved with her. We have not become victorious in our own strength. It was the prayers and arms of our beloved friends and family that lifted us up into the presence of the Almighty God for Him to make us victorious. Our pastors and their wives, cell leaders and cell members became friends, begging God on our behalf to send manna, then collecting it, helping us to become strong. Dark clouds that the enemy sent to engulf us were driven away by the love of family and friends. One day when heaven's gates will open for us, we will enter by the blood of Jesus Christ and because of the prayers, love and touch of the many people who have upheld us.

Sixty-six operations were all done in Pretoria, South Africa. For three years we traveled 600 km from Durban and for 11 years 1500 km from Zimbabwe.

After each operation Resje's stitches had to be removed. While living in Durban, our plastic surgeon suggested we ask our GP to perform the task, avoiding a return journey. This procedure was extremely traumatic for Resje but because of multiple general anaesthetics for surgery, additional administrations for the removal of the stitches were strongly discouraged. Our family doctor in Durban was a wonderful man. The day after she was born he came to visit me. He came in, sat on my bed, took my hand and started crying with me. He didn't say anything. We both sat there crying. Apart from Charl, he was the very first of many people who cried with me.

Resje was eight months old when the plastic surgeon in Pretoria took her on as patient. The first operation resulted in about 150 stitches. We took her to our GP in Durban. He summed up the situation and declared that there was no chance that he would be able to remove them without anaesthetics. I silently asked: "What now, God?" A voice from the back of the room quietly said: "If you give me the equipment to remove the clips, I'll do it". I turned. It was the voice of Resje's dad, my husband, Charl. His school holiday work with the local vet and his military medical training in Zimbabwe had prepared him to remove stitches. And for the next 66 operations, Charl removed the sutures, becoming proficient to the extent that the plastic surgeon would ask Charl's opinion and advice.

This was not an easy job for Charl. A friend and I would keep Resje as still as possible while he worked with the clip remover. Often Charl used only his one hand, helping the two of us to keep her still with his other hand. She was unbelievably strong, fighting us all the time, screaming continuously at the top of her voice. Charl calmly concentrated with a steady hand on the sutures, not being outwardly affected by her piercing screams. He would hug and kiss her once he was finished, showed her all the stitches he removed, commenting on how brave she was, and then he would disappear for hours, to come back with broken eyes.

At the age of fifteen a plastic surgeon in New Zealand did eleven skin grafts on her during a four-hour operation. This was her first operation in a new country. Nobody knew anything about her. That night, five hours after the operation, she told the nurse that she wanted to get up and walk to the bathroom by herself. The nurse ran out, we thought to fetch a wheel chair. As always, I pushed the pole with the intravenous drip and the catheter. When we reached the passage, we realized what the nurse had done. She had called the rest of the staff in the ward to come and look at a miracle. They stood there watching a determined teenager trying not to lose out on life. She smiled at them, they responded by clapping their hands. They clapped continuously. We walked past them, slowly, progressing inch by inch – but walking into the bathroom and heard them from there carrying on clapping. Through tears, I could hear the angels clapping their wings, watching proudly how God's creation fights her way out of pain and suffering.

The best psychological advice we were given was when Charl and I went to see a psychologist in Durban after Resje was born. Our family doctor, who cried with me when Resje was born, referred us to the psychologist. She explained to us that when Resje grew up we should allow her to verbalize her feelings about her skin condition whenever she felt the need to talk about it. We should not give her any advice during these sessions; because that is the day she needs us to listen to her. When she cries, we should cry with her. I have always tried to put this into practice. Resje has a few days a year where she collapses for a few hours in tears. I will stop everything I am doing, listen to her aching heart and I will cry with my daughter. God has been wonderfully good to us, but there are certain times in life where you have to face your hurts, acknowledge them, cry, grieve and mourn over them. Crying with Resje has permitted me to bond with her pain. Being allowed to verbalize her feelings has given her an enormous gift of coming into contact with her innermost soul, and in turn, reaching out to the depths of other people's souls.

Whenever people hear about the number of Resje's operations, they ask how many operations more or when they will end. I wish I had an answer. In many ways, Resje's life is as normal as everyone else's. She walks and runs. Since the age of seven, she has swum and enjoyed the sun. She laughs and plays, she loves helping in the kitchen but hates tidying her room, she loves to read and listens to music. When she is dressed in winter clothes, nobody notices anything. She has a number of small beauty spots on her face. They are a bit bigger than freckles and black, but they do not appear abnormal. It is when her arms and legs are uncovered that the scars and the naevi are visible. Her neck, back and lower back are the areas most affected.

Looking past the naevi and scars is her courageous and brave heart. What she suffers from now is the irritation. To her the scarring is virtually nothing. She is constantly aware of the itching, even in her sleep and it takes a huge amount of effort and discipline not to scratch when in public. Once she starts scratching, she will not stop until it bleeds. As always, the scratching brings only temporary relief.

The cup that she drinks out of now is to live with this irritating, itching sensation. This is a constant reminder that we are here to glorify and praise God whatever our circumstances. She does not have the physical strength to drink out of this cup. She is aware that it is by the power of the Holy Spirit of Jesus Christ that she swallows the content. The cup that I must drink out of is still the same cup that was given to me almost 27 years ago. I can only look upon her and am still not able to take her suffering away from her. But praise God, He has given me eyes to see Him standing at her side, holding her in His arms, lifting the cup for her, letting the

Holy Spirit go down with the content. Whenever I turn away with tears in my eyes, He is there with me, with tear-filled eyes, finding it extremely difficult to gaze upon her suffering too.

When Resje was 15 years old, she wrote the following:

Most people today are actors or actresses; whether or not they want to be. We all hide what we truly feel and we tell ourselves it is all right. We hide our pain in the deepest depths of our hearts and continue as if nothing has happened. We believe that if no one sees the pain, then no one will open up the past wounds. The pain hurts but we are too scared to confide in someone just how much it hurts.

Somewhere along the way, my mind became twisted. I pushed away the people who came forward to help me cope with the pain, thinking they were the ones who would hurt me the most. People, in their efforts to help, sometimes opened up past emotional wounds that at times had become infected. This hurt more than the new wounds because past wounds have already bled and hurt. Sometimes the sepsis of past wounds would pour out; tainting everything it touched. But always, opening past wounds would bring back the memories of receiving them. These memories haunted me.

Since I was little I have had an urgency to get away as quickly as possible from the hospital after each operation. I thought if I could just get away from the hospital, then my hurt would also disappear. The pain was still there but I felt that at least those who had the ability to hurt me had been left behind. I had come to believe that the hospital was not a place of healing but rather a place of torture.

It became increasingly obvious to me that it was necessary for some past scars to be opened and dealt with in order to go forward. I had to open up the wounds that were infected and rotten. The sepsis and filth within the wounds had to be cleaned out and the wounds closed. But I could not do this alone; I needed help. However; I was stubborn and refused to ask for help from anyone in case they, too, turned around and hurt me in some manner. I had always needed to walk, as soon as possible after an operation; so that if needed, I could get away from those who had caused the pain. I needed to get up to convince myself that I was not dead but only wounded and alive. I needed to protect myself from others.

I detested falseness in people looking at me with false compassion as if I was unable to do anything myself. I wanted to feel like a normal person, desiring space. It felt as if the whole world was staring at me. I wanted to hide from the world, not wanting to go out in the open where people could see me. I wanted to protect myself from the hurt I received from people who thought I was some kind of alien from outer space and that they needed protection from me. I often wanted to shout: "I'm human. I have feelings too."

I felt betrayed. I had not done anything to deserve this nor had I chosen this road. Why would I? Why would anyone choose a road of suffering? Did God allow this? If so, why did He choose me? If He was all-powerful then why did He not stop the suffering? Why does He write in the Bible that He loves me unconditionally, and then puts me on this road of suffering? I was confused. To make matters worse everyone had their own interpretation of why this happened and they tried to make me believe that their explanation was right. No one took the time to deal with me as a person but rather gave their explanations and then walked off. I felt alone. God gave me this cross to carry and then left me alone. Although I was little; I was required to carry this load. Forget companionship on this road. Life is tough but it is something that you have to do on your own, unless you are fortunate which I was not about to become. This was the way my life would be until I breathed my last breath. Some days I could not wait for that last breath, then all this pain and suffering would be over.

Every time there was a shimmer of hope of medical progress and physical relief, this hope was shattered. It was a vicious cycle of hope, hurt and disappointment. I had to accept that I was not going to be relieved of this burden. I was hurt and disappointed that God, allowed this to happen. He made me walk this road. It felt as if God had deserted me.

I did not believe He loved me. I justified my thinking by saying, everyone has their own amount of suffering; my level must not be that significant. Therefore God had simply put me aside, deeming me and my suffering unimportant. No one was watching to see if God was going to heal me. He had put me at the back of His mind and every year He would just think of me, wince and then say: "I have more important things to do than deal with her!"

I got angry with God. I struggled with the concept that He was in control of every situation. He did not seem to be in control of my situation. I blamed a lot on God. Every hurt I had ever received was His mistake. Every scar reminded me of His seemingly ignorance of what was happening to me. Every operation became a reminder that God had not healed me, every day a reminder of what He had not done. He did not care and He did not want to be involved in my life. I wondered why I was still reaching out to Him for healing if He was not going to be involved with me. Why not just leave Him, turn my back on Him and look after myself. It felt as if I had been looking after myself anyway without God's help. It hurt like crazy but then it made more sense than trusting God who did not want anything to do with me.

I subconsciously put up a wall that I believed was indestructible and impenetrable to protect myself from the hurt. I spent hours trying to convince myself I did not need the painkillers while my body seared with pain. I excelled at hiding pain from those I loved, not wanting to hurt them. It took me a while to realize that this was not something I was going to be able to cope with alone. I needed someone, but whom?

The person I needed had to be someone I could explode at times without him/her getting angry at me and then at other times it needed to be someone who would just hold me as the tears kept falling. Someone who did not mind the stench of the festered wounds. Someone who would always be there. I needed someone who understood the pain the way I felt it, not someone who lost a leg or whose parents split up when they were young. I needed someone who knew how it felt to have my pain - my individual pain.

One night after an operation I looked out of the window. I saw a broken, battered and bruised Man. He stretched out His hand and I took it. That night I found the Person who could identify with my individual pain -Jesus Christ. He was there every single minute of each day. He not only knew the kind of pain I had, but also how my heart hurt. He did not mind the sepsis, the filth, the blood, the open wounds and the scar tissue. I did not have to act in front of Him and pretend that it was all right, so as not to hurt His feelings. I did not have to hold my tongue when I was angry or upset. He is a rock of strength when the world comes crashing down. He forgives me even when I say things in the heat of anger that could destroy the best of friendships. But, most important of all I know He does not see my scars. He sees the true me, the one inside my scarred body. And He loves me.

Because of Resje's suffering, I was denied the normal joys of motherhood. When I breastfed Resje, she sucked at me with such fervor to try and find some relief from the agonizing pain, that I never felt I nourished her. Bathing her was a quick process of getting her in and out of water. Everything added to her irritation: the water, soap and towels. To change her nappies and clothes meant she would lie down on the carpet and wriggle like a snake, tearing open her flesh. Clean nappies and clothes had to be quickly put on to prevent her from hurting herself. There was little time to cuddle her, or to permit her to discover and explore her body. Hugs were gentle and soft, so as not to hurt her. Our games were limited. I was always afraid she might tear her stitches, which she did regularly. I was forever saying: "Don't run, mind there, let me pick you up, be careful."

I was more a nurse to her, than a mother. She had wounds all the time. My priority was to look after the wounds, change her dressings, watch the stitches, monitor the infection and forcing down antibiotics.

Other moms would share ideas about various foods for their babies or discuss different exercises; I would think about how we were going to cope with 150 stainless steel clips in her body. Other moms boasted about new development stages in their babies; I would wonder how I was going to pick her up without hurting her. Other moms complained about their lack of sleep; my night consisted of two hours and if I was very lucky two more hours much later in the night. On average, other moms fell pregnant two to three years after their first child; I wondered how I would ever have enough energy and strength to survive another operation. Other moms complained about teething; I fought away the threat of malignant melanoma.

Four months after Resje turned seven, the surgeon removed the entire naevus on her back, alleviating about 80% of the irritation. I began to breathe. Five months later, I turned forty. I thought although the time is not perfect for a second child, and Resje is not completely healed, it is now or never. I wanted another girl. When nothing happened the first month, I was not surprised; to be honest I was quite relieved. Then nothing happened the second, the third, the fourth month, the whole year and the next year. I went to God. He took me to four women in His Word.

The first woman was Hannah. It was the same name as my mother, causing me to connect immediately with Hannah in the Bible. Hannah could not conceive but after Eli had prayed for her, she gave birth to Samuel. Then God took me to a nameless woman, the wife of Manoah. The Bible never mentions her name so that her identity remains a secret. I immediately identified with her. I, too, felt as if I had lost my identity as a person, being only the mother and nurse of Resje. This nameless woman could not conceive. An angel of the Lord appeared to her and gave her the promise of having a child, Samson, whom she subsequently had. Lastly, God took me to Sarah and Elizabeth. They were both barren and old. The Bible says of Sarah that she was past the age of childbearing and of Elizabeth that she was well advanced in years. I thought I was like them; I was becoming well advanced in years for a woman wanting a child. After the promises given to them by the Angel of the Lord, Sarah gave birth to Isaac and Elizabeth to John.

In all four cases the women were given boys from God. It dawned upon me. God wanted to give me a boy. That was why I could not fall pregnant. Then, during one visit to the gynaecologist in Zimbabwe, he told me that I had six more months in which to fall pregnant before giving up on having a second child. Three months before turning forty-five, I sat down with God. I had to sacrifice yet another dream. I gave Him my desire for a girl, willing to accept a little boy from Him, if that was His will. I fell pregnant that same month.

Resje was ecstatic. She discovered the magazines and books on pregnancy that I had bought years before when I was pregnant with her. I had never even looked at them, now Resje was studying them. At first she asked me questions. Later, I consulted her on maternity matters. We laughed a lot and together bought baby clothes. We could not stop feeling the new life. She spoke to the baby, welcoming him to her world.

I learned from her how to relax and love the unborn baby. She was proud of my expanding stomach, showing it off to her friends, explaining to me the miracle of life, showing me how to accept this tremendous gift from God.

I was not only pregnant with this baby - Resje's enthusiasm began growing in me. Her excitement and joy cancelled out the dark feelings I had when I was pregnant with her. I relived my first pregnancy, acting it out in reality, this time with love and hope, joy and happiness.

When I was forty-five years old, and Resje a mature twelve, our baby boy was born.

The doctor allowed Resje to come into the delivery room seconds after the baby was born. She held him before his dad and I had the opportunity. That night in the hospital bed, I could not take my eyes off my little boy. God had given me a little boy, Emil, because it was His will. He was a blessing and a gift from God. He was healthy and perfect. His skin was normal. I was a mother.

Sarah called her boy Isaac meaning laughter:
> "God has made me laugh, and all who hear will laugh with me." (Genesis 21:6, NKJ)

This was a happy laughter; their hearts were filled with joy. That was how I felt. My heart overflowed with joy. I could not stop smiling at the baby. It was a first for me to experience the normal joys of motherhood. From now on I would also worry about ordinary things. Did the baby drink enough? Was he sleeping? Was he wet? Should I bath him? I would be able to hug his little body close to mine and cuddle him, play and laugh with him.

The next day we went back to the farm. It was a two-hour drive. Resje held the baby as if he was the most precious thing on earth. He was. He was a human being, a male child, a little boy and a gift from God.

It was amazing to see how Resje was involved with her brother. She was a young mother when she bathed and clothed him, a little girl when she played with him. I realized she was reliving her toddler years - this time without plaster casts, running, rolling and jumping freely with her brother. In addition, God gave me the joy of witnessing this.

She asked hundreds of questions: Was she like this? Did she do it this way? Did I also tickle her like this?

From the moment her brother was born, he bonded with his big sister. He grew up watching her going to hospital, seeing her suffering. He does not see the scars or the remaining naevi; he sees her heart. He does not panic when she scratches herself until she bleeds. She is his big, brave sister. To him she is beautiful; he loves and adores her. He loves her long hair. She is sometimes a second mommy to him; at other times she is his best playmate. The one moment she protects him; the next moment she teases him. This is his sister's face, her arms and legs, her hands and feet, her back and neck. He prays every day to God, asking Him to give his sister a new skin. However, when he looks at her, he sees her. He sees her love and encouragement, her gentleness and caring nature; he sees her beauty and her graciousness, the brave and courageous heart of a lioness and he is so proud of his big sister.

From the most selfish person in the world, I changed to a mother whose two children are my greatest earthly joys. The two of them are my blessed heritage from God; they are my precious reward, my fierce arrows. Oh, who am I that God would bless me this much!

I often read the Book of Job in the Bible. I guess I have found the ultimate suffering in Job. It is not difficult to see Job, sitting in the midst of the ashes with a potsherd with which to scrape him. Resje has done this. She is still doing this. Her potsherd is her fingers, nails and knuckles. We keep her nails short, to limit the damage. She clenches her fists and uses her knuckles as a potsherd to scratch the hard scar tissue. Often the skin on her knuckles wears through. Her bedroom and the bathroom are her ashes. She will smile to everyone in the lounge and then disappear to her ashes. I will find her there, sitting in a heap, not aware of time or place, with an anguished face, trying to find a little bit relief. Blood will ooze out of the scratched wounds and she will apologize for the blood on her clothes, the blood on the sheets, the blood on the floor.

Like Job and by the grace of God, Resje and I will never give up on God. We know He is real and He will never leave nor forsake us. We do not always understand Him, but we both trust and love Him with all our hearts. He is the Lord of our lives and we submit to Him and His will. We both believe in miracles and that God will one day give her a new skin. We yearn for that day, but we both have learned to live in the present and to accept every new day as a gift from God. Resje prays every morning, thanking God that He has chosen to give her one more day to live in His presence.

We have both come to realize and to accept that God is more important to us than a healthy skin.

I especially turn to the Book of Job when feeling a bit low. Then I skip the pages where Job sits with his potsherd, and go straight to the end of Job where God starts healing and restoring Job, blessing him with more than he previously had. I love to read Job 42:15:

> "In all the land were found no women so beautiful as the daughters of Job."(NKJ)

I look upon my slain girl, past her outward appearance right into her heart. I have toured through Europe, I have lived in South Africa, Zimbabwe, New Zealand and Australia, and I can honestly say in all the many countries I have been I have found no woman as beautiful as my precious Resje.

Chapter Ten

THE SUN OF RIGHTEOUSNESS
(Healing and restoration of our marriage)

"But to you who fear My name the Sun of Righteousness shall arise with healing in His wings; and you shall go out and grow fat like stall-fed calves.

You shall trample the wicked, for they shall be ashes under the soles of your feet on the day that I do this." (Malachi 4:2-3, NKJ)

"And the Lord God said, 'It is not good that man should be alone; I will make him a helper comparable to him.'

Out of the ground the Lord God formed every beast of the field and every bird of the air, and brought them to Adam to see what he would call them. And whatever Adam called each living creature, that was its name.

So Adam gave names to all cattle, to the birds of the air, and to every beast of the field. But for Adam there was not found a helper comparable to him.

And the Lord God caused a deep sleep to fall on Adam, and he slept; and He took one of his ribs, and closed up the flesh in its place.

> Then the rib which the Lord God had taken from man He made into a woman, and He brought her to the man.
>
> And Adam said:
>
> 'This is now bone of my bones and flesh of my flesh;
>
> She shall be called Woman, because she was taken out of man.'
>
> Therefore a man shall leave his father and mother and be joined to his wife, and they shall become one flesh."
> (Genesis 2:18-24, NKJ)

A friend of mine worked in the Paediatric Oncology unit in Durban, South Africa. In many cases the parents who brought their sick children there never saw their children healed. I remember her words describing the trauma of parents trying to cope with the shock and pain of a dying child. At the onset of treatment the parents would be together supporting their child. Then over a period of time some parents would visit separately. After a while many of them would separate or divorce.

In the world we are living in, we want to experience everything with our senses. We want to see the enemy because we look at the world with physical eyes. We perceive cancer and any other trauma as something abstract. Instead of uniting against the real enemy, parents turn against each other and fight. It is easier to fight your partner, who you observe physically, than to fight something abstract. This is precisely what the devil wants. If he can manage to turn us against the people around us he succeeds in breaking up relationships and that is his main aim.

We read in the Bible that when a man leaves his parents and cleaves to his wife, "they shall become one flesh" (Genesis

2:24). By implication this means a man and a woman alone is only half of this biblical principle. We read:

> "So God created man in His own image; in the image of God He created him; male and female He created them." (Genesis 1:27, NKJ)

A man and a woman are the two components of the image of God. Because God embodies both genders, He fully understands us. God can be your intimate friend because He understands your gender. He is also your lover because He embodies the opposite sex. He is simultaneously our protecting Father, providing for us as well as being our caring mother, nourishing us.

We have complicated relationships by looking for all these different attributes in our spouses. It is a foolish exercise, for they do not possess all these attributes. Only God encompasses this whole. Our marriage partners can never be a friend, lover, father, mother or protector simultaneously. However, when a man and woman unite in marriage, the godly characteristics of a man and the godly characteristics of a woman can bring forth the characteristics and qualities of God. Two separate entities become one whole, created in God's image. We sometimes look for something in our spouses that can only surface when we are in unity.

When God did not take the suffering of Resje away, I looked to Charl to do God's work. I wanted him to be the image of God to us, to be our saviour, healer and protector. He had to save us from the enemy of suffering and protect us from the hurt and pain. I wanted him to have all the answers, to listen to and counsel me, to restore my world and bring hope and life to Resje's. Of course he could not do it. I knew consciously I could never expect this from him and that this thinking was absurd and ridiculous. But I kept dreaming and hoping for a magical world of painlessness and wanted Charl to rescue us from the harsh reality, bringing us into a kingdom of peace and painlessness. I wanted Charl to be a saviour and god not only to Resje but also to myself.

The same psychologist who told us that we should listen to Resje's cries from her heart and not console her with empty words, told us that the two of us should always share our burdens with one another, because a "burden shared is a burden halved". We listened to her advice and believed in this principle; however, both of us could not apply it. It was impossible to off-load some of my burden onto Charl, seeing how difficult it was for him to cope with his burden. He was the same. He thought I had so much to carry that he was not going to make it more difficult for me.

In the beginning we shared and spoke about Resje's suffering, not our own, and then we stopped. Life does not come to a halt when something happens, whether it is good or bad. Life expects you to get over a thing and move on, which is what we both wanted. Neither of us wanted to stagnate or complain the whole time. We found it difficult to find that fine balance between complaining and off-loading by sharing. In our eagerness in wanting to move on, and in our desire not to hurt one another more than we were already hurt, we missed out on sharing our burdens.

We were two broken, defeated individuals trying to cope with suffering. We were two halves that needed to unite before we could look at the invasion of suffering in our lives.

It was only after I got to know God as my spiritual husband that I realized I was expecting the impossible from Charl. I had to accept that a healed, victorious, and restored Charl would always be only one half of what God intended for us to be. In unity, we could rise up and become the image of God. I had to repent again, amazed at my own lack of understanding and surprised at yet another idol in my life. Charl was never going to be able to deliver and heal us. Only God could give me what I yearned for. No human being on earth could fulfill the deep desires of my heart.

When God reveals something, forgiveness is nearly always the second step. I found it very difficult to forgive Charl for not being able to destroy the enemy in our lives until I realized I was making two huge mistakes. Firstly, it was not Charl that I needed to forgive - I needed to forgive myself! I was the one who wanted to turn him into a god, wanting him to possess all the attributes of God. Charl never tried to be a god - he remained true to his own human nature with his human strengths and weaknesses. I wanted the impossible from him. I needed to forgive myself from the desire to turn him into a god and had to release him from my expectation to deliver us from suffering.

The second mistake I made was that I had the wrong perspective of who the real enemy was. For many years I thought Resje's suffering was our enemy and that I had to fight it. When she was little I thought I would never accept this skin condition, thinking we would conquer it, destroy it and cut it out of her body. I perceived her suffering to be the cause of a strenuous marriage. Charl's failure to beat the enemy of suffering reflected to me his inability to be the warrior I wanted him to be. When the day came that I realized it was her suffering that brought me to God, I embraced it with open arms. The moment I embraced it, I gave God a tool in His hands to bring life to us. Suffering was not the enemy. The enemy was the devil laughing at us with the many tools we gave him - lack of intimacy, silence, tiredness, hopelessness, anger, bitterness, frustration and irritation. The devil was trying to destroy our relationship so that we could "profane the Lord's holy institution which He loves" and to prevent us from having "godly offspring" (Malachi 2:11-16).

Having gone through a divorce once before I found myself (especially in the early years of marriage) thinking thoughts like: "I've blown it again; this is it - you can't make a man happy; divorce number two coming up; the devil's won again; this would never work", and on and on I went. Praise God that Charl on the other hand reacted in the opposite way. He took his marriage vows seriously. To him, marriage was holy. It might be difficult, and boy, did I make it difficult for him at times, but he had married me for better and for worse. He would be upset and angry with me, but he would stay put. I was not going to get rid of him. He was in my life to stay, whether I liked it or not, until death do us part and further to provide for Resje and for me, to pray for us and to love us.

And that is exactly what he has done all these years. He has stood by us and prayed for us. God in His infinite wisdom hovered over all the men on earth to find the perfect husband for me and father for Resje. He found Charl and sent him to me. No other man would have been able to persevere like he did and no other man would have been able to pick us up and carry us through the fiery furnace like he did. God did send me a warrior. Selflessly he fought silently, day and night, year after year, operation after operation, for his wife and his child. He has never given up on us and by the grace of God he never will.

One of God's principles is that He works in seasons. He created a season for everything. When it is the season of mourning we want to get it over with as soon as possible. We forget that God ordained it for a time. We are surrounded by a physical and material world urging us on to move onward and expand our boundaries. Often that is in direct opposition to the inner world of God wanting us to come to terms with the gifts He has put on our path of life. To explore the seasons of God takes time and effort and it requires patience and sharing, growing inwardly and expanding the walls of our hearts. We read:

> "To everything there is a season, a time for every purpose under heaven:

A time to be born, and a time to die;

A time to plant, and a time to pluck what is planted;

A time to kill, and a time to heal;

A time to break down, and a time to build up;

A time to weep, and a time to laugh;

A time to mourn, and a time to dance;

A time to cast away stones, and a time to gather stones;

A time to embrace, and a time to refrain from embracing;

A time to gain, and a time to lose;

A time to keep, and a time to throw away;

A time to tear, and a time to sew;

A time to keep silence, and a time to speak;

A time to love, and a time to hate;

A time of war, and a time of peace."

(Ecclesiastes 3:1-8, NKJ)

God gave me a husband and a child to take me through several seasons. During some seasons I felt far from God; during others I was filled with anger and despair. Then He sent me the Creator of the seasons. I turned to find Him standing at the top of Mount Zion in front of the tree of life. Like Charl, He took His marriage vows to me, a sinner, seriously. To Him, marriage was holy, He married me for better and for worse and He was in my life to stay.

This caused me to identify the real enemy and to look differently at God. The real enemy was the devil trying his best to ruin our relationship. He did not want us to reach our full potential or that we should come to the knowledge that we were created in the image of God. However, by His grace God revealed Himself to me, wanting something different for us. This is what He wanted:

> "Therefore, just as the church is subject to Christ, so let the wives be to their own husbands in everything.
>
> Husbands, love your wives, just as Christ also loved the church and gave Himself for her,
>
> that He might sanctify and cleanse her with the washing of water by the word,
>
> that He might present her to Himself a glorious church, not having spot or wrinkle or any such thing, but that she should be holy and without blemish.
>
> So husbands ought to love their own wives as their own bodies; he who loves his wife loves himself.
>
> For no one ever hated his own flesh, but nourishes and cherishes it, just as the Lord does the church.
>
> For we are members of His body, of His flesh and of His bones." (Ephesians 5:24-30, NKJ)

Resje carried tumours, spots and blemishes on her skin. The way to get rid of that was through cutting it out. We carried spots and blemishes in our hearts and in our marriage. The only way to get rid of that was by the washing of water by the Word. The healing of our marriage depended on God, sanctifying and cleansing us by His Word. We had to stay in His Word, studying and meditating on it. The more I tried to find God's purpose in Resje's suffering through studying the Word, the more God cleansed my heart with the washing of water by the Word. I was stunned when I realized the blessing her suffering brought once again. Resje's suffering caused me to study God's Word. By studying God's Word, His Word was cleansing and washing me, bringing healing to my broken soul. Resje was amazing. God used her suffering to heal and restore my womanhood, my motherhood and now our marriage.

When we look at God's mathematical principles we find the principle of multiplication at work:

> "How could one chase a thousand, and two put ten thousand to flight, unless their Rock had sold them and the Lord had surrendered them?"
>
> (Deuteronomy 32:30, NKJ)

Unity is very important to God. One alone can achieve in a limited way, however when two people unite there is a multiplication by ten that comes into effect. A tremendous blessing from God rests on the unison:

> "Behold, how good and how pleasant it is for brethren to dwell together in unity!
>
> It is like the precious oil upon the head, running down on the beard, the beard of Aaron, running down on the edge of his garments.
>
> It is like the dew of Hermon, descending upon the mountains of Zion; for there the Lord commanded the blessing – life forevermore." (Psalm 133, NKJ)

God wants to bestow on us His anointing and life the moment we unite. What more could we ask for? With His anointing we could remain standing in the presence of the devil, sending the roaring toothless lion into hiding.

When Adam looked at Eve for the first time he proclaimed:

> "This is now bone of my bones and flesh of my flesh;
>
> She shall be called Woman, because she was taken out of man." (Genesis 2:23, NKJ)

I realized the purpose of humankind when I read:

> "For we are members of His body, of His flesh and of His bones." (Ephesians 5:30, NKJ)

The first Adam was alone and lonely, without a helper comparable to him. The same happened with the second Adam - Jesus. During a deep sleep God took one of Adam's ribs from his side to make Adam a companion and helper suitable to reign with him. When Jesus died, His side was pierced. Water and blood poured from His side. As with the first Adam, Father God sent darkness so that the earth could fall into a deep sleep. From that water and blood God now creates a companion and helper for His Son. The moment we are baptized with water, claiming the blood of Jesus over our sins a new creation arises. When this new breed of people, the believers in Jesus Christ unite, we will have the characteristics of God and become the image of Almighty God, our living King. That is the day that Jesus Christ will come down from the heavens to fetch us, His bride, to look us in the eye and say: 'My bride, now you are bone of My bones and flesh of My flesh.' What a tremendous honour and privilege to one day be part of the bones and the flesh of Jesus Christ and to reign with Him! What does it matter if our temporary outward shells have holes or tumours in it? If it causes us to turn away from God, it is cursed. However, if our broken bodies and shattered lives lead us to the bones and flesh of our Saviour, it is the biggest blessing in the universe.

As God is busy refining me, He wants me to become part of the bones and flesh of Jesus Christ. Daily I have to crucify my own desires, to learn from and adapt to Jesus' desires, needs and wants. When the church of Jesus Christ one day unites and succeeds in crucifying its own desires, plans and schemes, Jesus Christ will appear to fetch His bride, proclaiming proudly that we are now bones of His bones, and flesh of His flesh.

My daughter's broken body and our shattered lives have miraculously, by His grace, caused the desire to cover our broken lives with an exquisite wedding dress. I prayed for years for a small miracle of the healing of an outward fleshly temporary condition. I almost missed the greatest miracle on earth – our salvation and rebirth into a Heavenly Kingdom, spending eternity with the God of our lives, the Lover of our souls and the Breath of our spirits. He healed our souls and spirits by His stripes, our names have been nailed into His Hands, He touched our hearts, He will one day wipe away all our many tears when He comes to relieve us from the itching and the irritation of our earthly lives.

Like the woman I know who sat at her table and had a vision of Jesus etched on her kitchen wall, I have seen Him too. If He had revealed Himself to me as the roaring lion that could heal Resje's skin with the snap of His fingers, my heart would have remained cold and stained, wanting people and circumstances to fulfill my flesh. Slowly, over many years, He revealed Himself to me as the slain Lamb. The slain Lamb had a life-changing effect on me. He revealed to me a part of my heart where I yearned for a magical life of praise and dancing, worshiping the Man of my life, a mighty God who created me, a loving Father leading and guiding me, a doting Husband loving me, a fierce Protector guarding my life, a generous Provider lavishing me with wine and bread, a caring Mother nourishing me, an intimate Friend understanding me, a Super-hero waiting to carry me off to eternal life.

Daily, He is fulfilling that yearning, gently stretching the part inside my heart, replacing my weak bones and my blemished flesh with His strong bones and His victorious flesh. I have come to know Him, to love Him and to fear Him. He is arising with healing in His wings. With anticipation I am waiting for Him to open the gate for me to go out, to trample the wicked as ashes under the soles of my feet.

It took more than twenty years for me to look past Resje's wounds, past her scars, her suffering and her pain. By God's grace I closed my eyes to wash away the mud and to look past the visible world. The eyes of my heart opened up wide to another time and place, to an invisible God real to my soul.

With outstretched arms He touched my ears to hear His breathing. He hovered over my chaotic life. His whispers spoke into my life, creating a new universe for me, filling it with His presence and His love. I came from Him, the Source of Life and one day I will return to Him.

But, praise God, I will not return with empty hands. I will have my earthly husband leading the way, my precious daughter dancing alongside me, and my son shouting with joy and victory when we meet our King of kings, and our Lord of lords.

EPILOGUE

God: How do you feel now?

I: I must admit I feel quite fragile.

God: My Kingdom is not from this world. If you are strong and powerful, I cannot help you. If you are successful and happy, you may not need me. That is why the poor and the sick, the needy and the outcasts are blessed in My Kingdom. They will look for me and find me. Once they have looked into My eyes, they will be changed.

I: It sounds as if Your Kingdom is not for the successful, wealthy, healthy and powerful people.

God: Unless you are born again, you cannot enter My Kingdom. It is not impossible for them. It is easier when you are in need, to look up at someone who can help you. If the wealthy and the successful look up, they will find me hovering over them, longing for them to find me.

I: If the rich and famous do not need You, why do You make them rich and successful? Is it not better for Your Kingdom that we all belong to You, glorifying You? What about people of other religions and beliefs? Could You not let them be born of Christian parents? Why do You only help the sick and the needy? What about all the people out there who think they do not need You?

God: Why do you ask me all these questions?

"… it was necessary for the Christ to suffer and to rise from the dead the third day, and that repentance and remission of sins should be preached in His name to all nations, beginning at Jerusalem. And you are witnesses of these things. Behold, I send the Promise of My Father upon you; but tarry in the city of Jerusalem until you are endued with power from on high."

(Luke 24:46-49, NKJ)

People keep asking where I am in the earthquakes, hurricanes and Tsunamis, where I am in poverty and success? The answers lie with you. I will tell you where I am. I am in you. I have given everyone who believes here on earth My Spirit to fill and empower him, to make him a child and representative of Me. Where am I in you, tell me, where am I?

I: You are in me, Lord, yet I lack something.

God: You want power and strength for yourself. It is not by power or might, but by My Spirit. I put you through the fiery furnace. You are precious to me. You know now at what cost I bought you.

I: The only thing the furnace did to me is to show me my flesh. I do not see any precious gems.

God: Then look through My eyes!

(As in a dream, I see a little girl eating a red apple in the midst of a group of children. She breaks the apple into pieces, giving it to her friends. Each time she puts a piece of apple into a friend's hand, it turns into a beautiful red ruby.

A boy with red hair approaches the little girl. He pulls her hair. I see the anger and hurt in her shoulders as she bends down to pick up the bundles of hair he pulled out. As she turns around to face the boy, forgiveness floods her eyes, changing her tender smile into pure white pearls. She picks up a bucket of water to wash away the dirt from the child's head and face. Throwing out the dirty water, something hard and shiny falls on the ground. She bends down to look at the glitter and sparkle of a huge, beautiful diamond.

The little girl grows up into a woman. Each time someone visits, she gives the person an ornament. As they leave the ornaments change into colourful and precious stones.)

God: Have you seen enough?

I: It is You who change our good deeds into precious gems.

God: Look further, see how close you are to the top of the mountain!

(I see an eagle, spreading her wings, gliding in the wind, circling the top of the mountain, flying higher and higher. She passes her nest, calling her children to follow her. The whole sky is filled with eagles: big and small, male and female, old and young. The wind carries them; effortless they soar higher and higher.)

God: Do you understand? I long for my precious bride, without spot or wrinkle to soar with me. I will wipe away the tears; exchange her beauty for ashes, the oil of joy for mourning and give her a garment of praise for the spirit of heaviness. I want to adorn her with jewels and gold, with silver and precious gems, with my love - warm and pure. You have tried to remove the black spots and tumours on your daughter's skin; I try to remove the black spots and tumours on my bride's heart.

I: I think I understand a little bit more, Lord. Because of Resje I looked up and found You. Through her agonizing cries, I heard You calling me. Her pain and suffering became the steps upwards to Your heavenly throne. You turned the curses in our lives into blessings. The curse of Resje's condition became a blessing to me. I know now that Your Kingdom is not from this world. I praise You and glorify Your name, honour and exalt You. Your joy is now my strength. You have turned my mourning into dancing, my stained spirit into sparkling jewels.

God: Oh, how I love you. I have given you my life. I love you more than you will ever know. I love you in all your ways. I have formed you. I love your heart and your soul. Now you are mine. Your name is written on the palm of My Hand. I am coming soon to take you with me. I have put My Spirit in you to lead and guide you, to never leave or forsake you. I have called you and you have heard My voice. You belong to Me:

" 'And behold, I am coming quickly, and My reward is with Me, to give to every one according to his work.

I am the Alpha and the Omega, the Beginning and the End, the First and the Last.'

Blessed are those who do His commandments, that they may have the right to the tree of life, and may enter through the gates into the city.

But outside are dogs and sorcerers and sexually immoral and murderers and idolaters, and whoever loves and practices a lie.

'I, Jesus, have sent My angel to testify to you these things in the churches. I am the Root and the Offspring of David, the Bright and Morning Star.'

And the Spirit and the bride say, 'Come!' And let him who hears say, 'Come!' And let him who thirsts come. Whoever desires, let him take the water of life freely."

(Revelation 22:12-17, NKJ)

I: I hear You whispering to Resje. It is good, Lord. Your timing is perfect. You should have the final word, addressing the precious girl of my life. I wanted You to speak to her long ago. Now You have opened her ears to hear Your breathing and opened the eyes of her heart to see You. You are hovering over the chaos of her irritated life. You are creating a new universe for her, filling it with Your presence and Your love. What are You saying to her, Lord?

God: I am saying to her what I have said to you, what I want to say to all my children. I live in you - it is time to arise. I am always with her. She is my unique work of art. Look, I am touching her now:

Talitha, cumi, My Resh, Talitha, cumi!

Our wedding day - oblivious to what lies ahead...

Resje's christening: A proud mom

A proud dad in love with his daughter

A mom in love with her daughter

My princess - a gift from God

My beautiful little girl - a long road of suffering, pain and anguish awaiting...

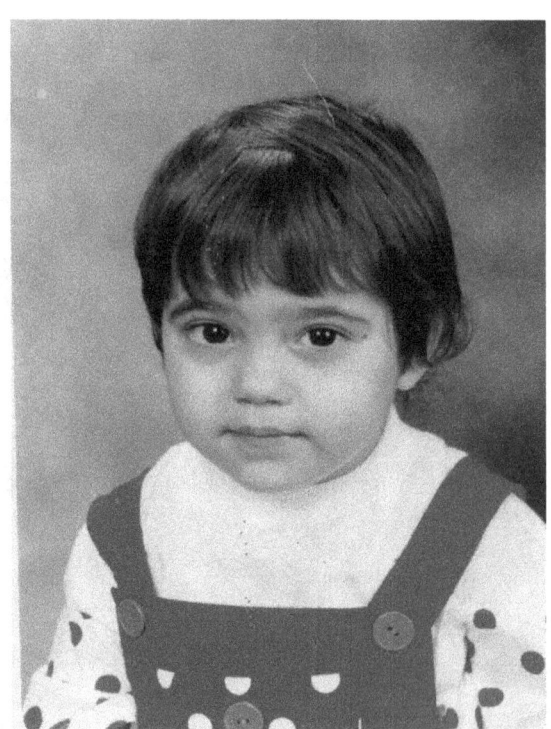

One of the most important men in Resje's life - my dad, her grandfather

Another one of the most important men in Resje's life - her doctor, Koos Scholtz

Dancing our sorrows away

My gorgeous darling

Resje and her baby brother, Emil

God is the Light in my life, Emil is the little light

God brought much healing and restoration through Emil

Enjoying the snow in New Zealand

My precious little girl turning 21 - Praise be to God who has given us an abundance of years!

A proud Charl at his daughter's graduation ceremony at the University of Otago in Dunedin, N.Z.

Like Sam in Lord of the Rings – I cannot carry your load or you anymore, my daughter, but I can be alongside you

The four of us in Australia

Resje -2012- the heartbeat of my life

1988 – Giant Pigmented Naevi

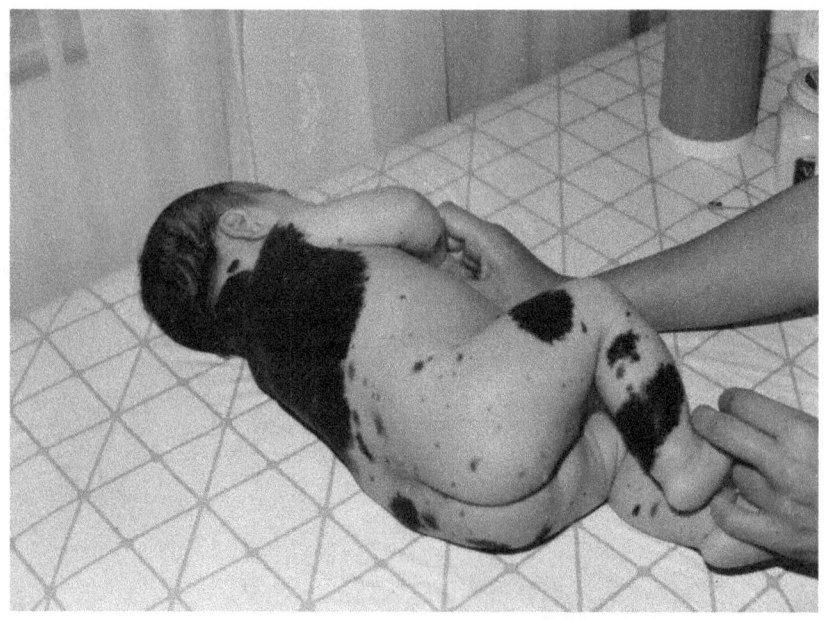

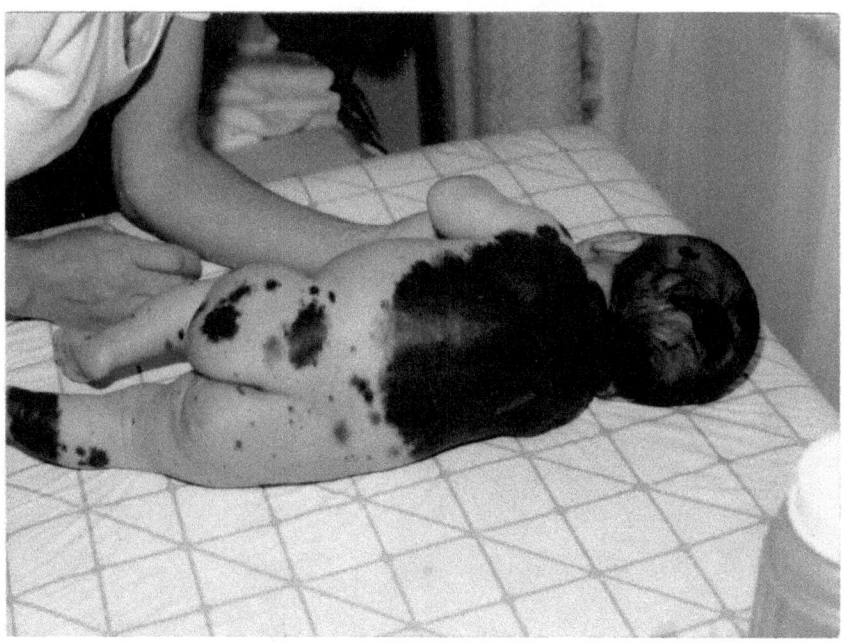

The evening before her first operation at six weeks

If only I could hide her pain…

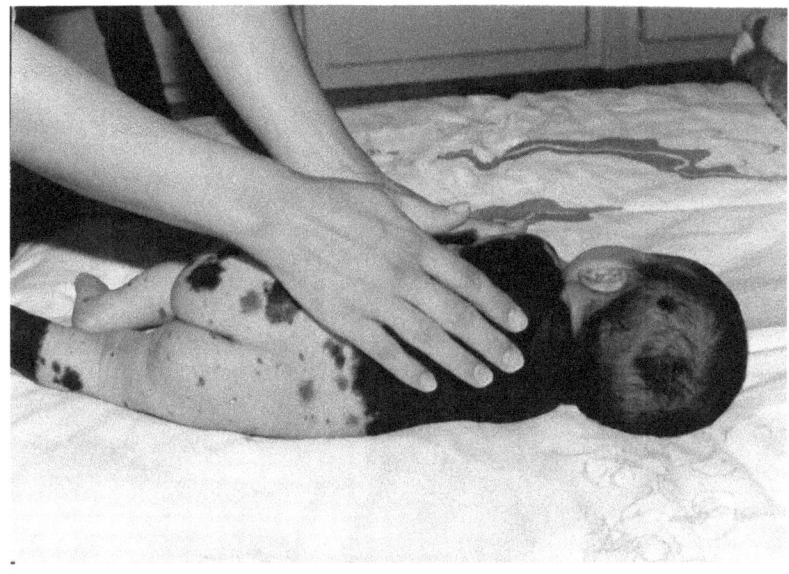

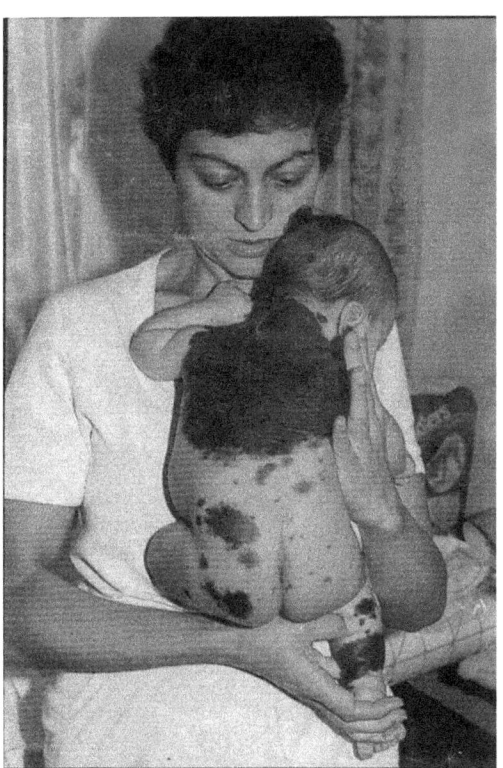

How could a beauty spot this big bring so much suffering…

God knew she had to be healthy and strong for the long road ahead

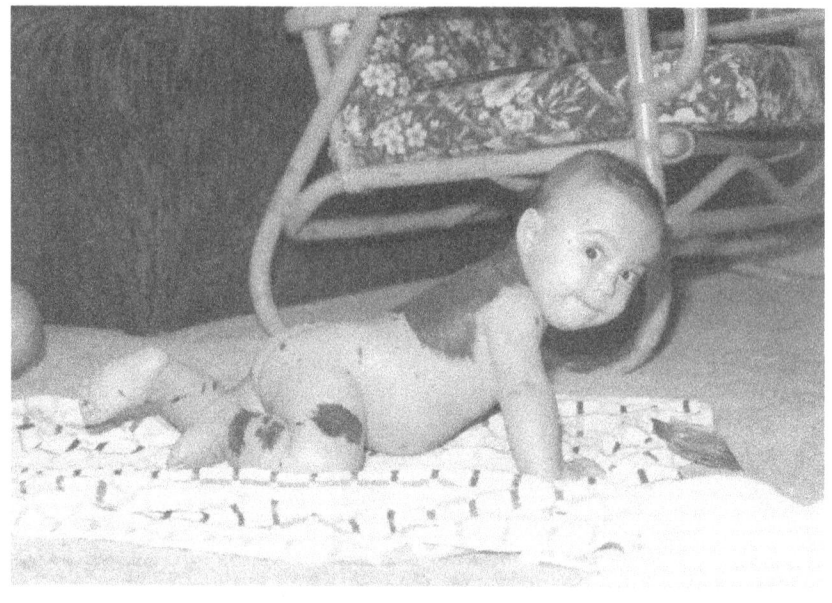

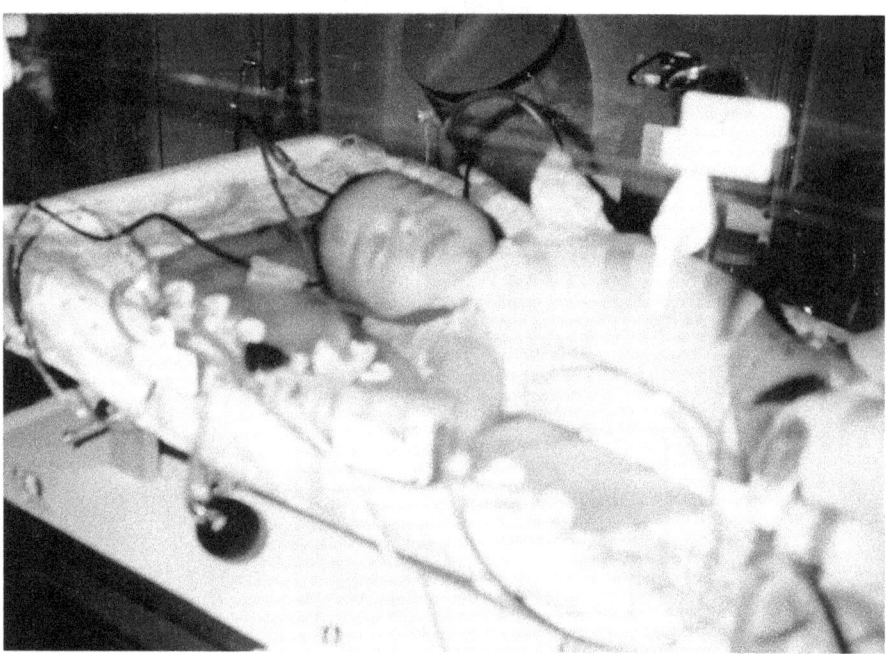

Her first operation at six weeks - she almost died

A concerned dad

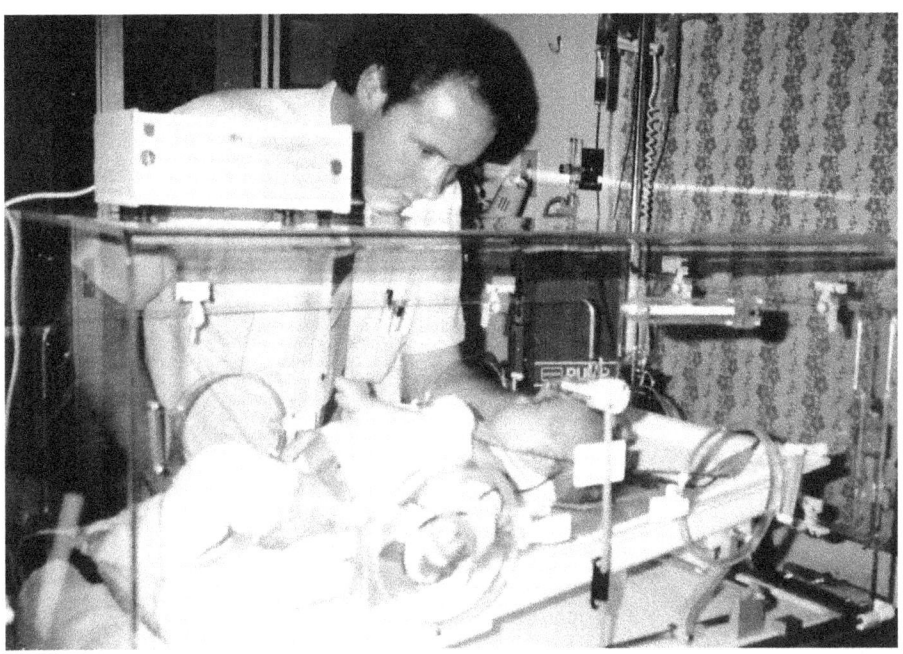

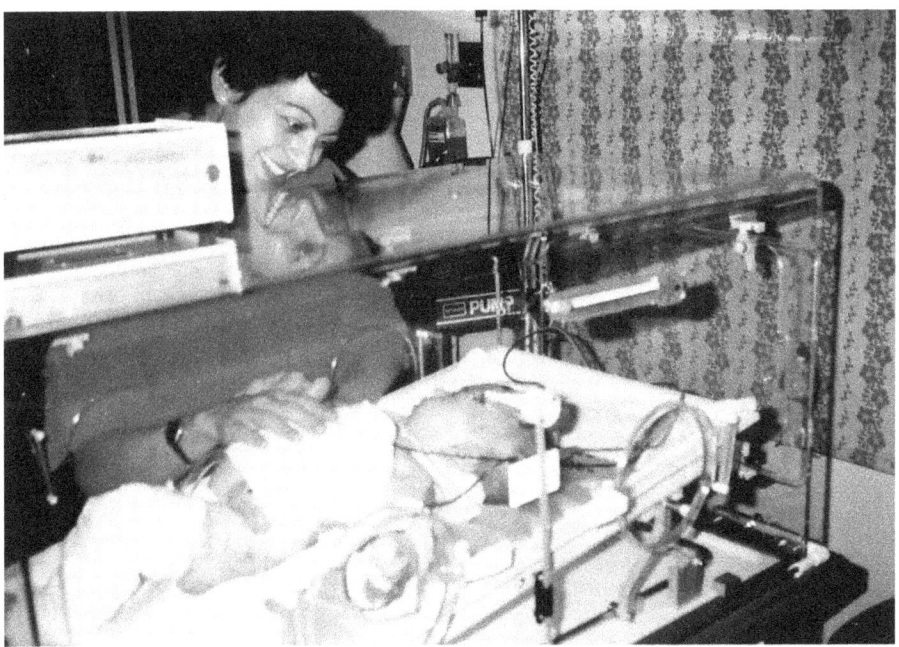

A mom trying to bring normalcy to a baby fighting for her life

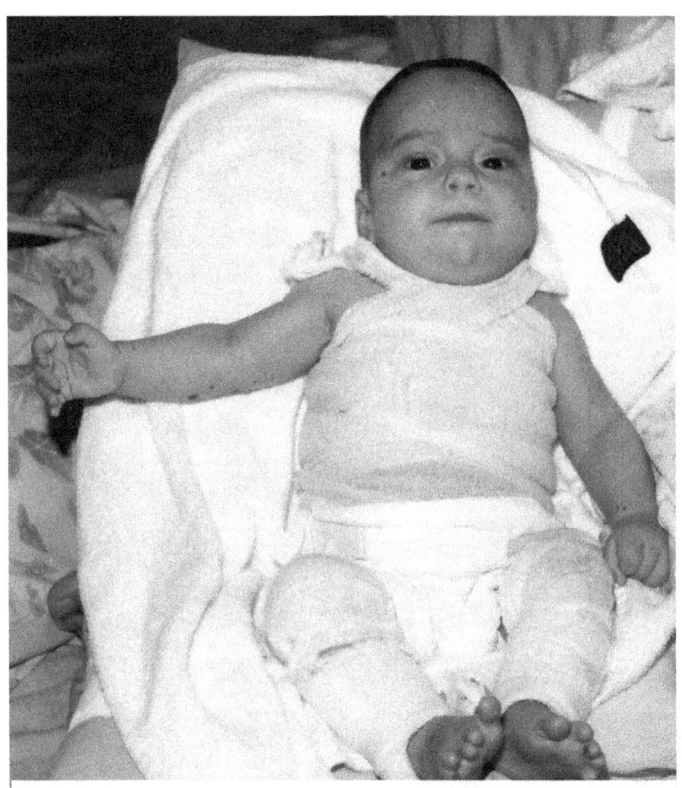

A baby in bandages – a standard set for the next two decades

An arm in bandage on her second birthday - Learning to blow out the candles

Jewellery is a girl's best friend! Her hand at its usual spot- hitting her neck or back

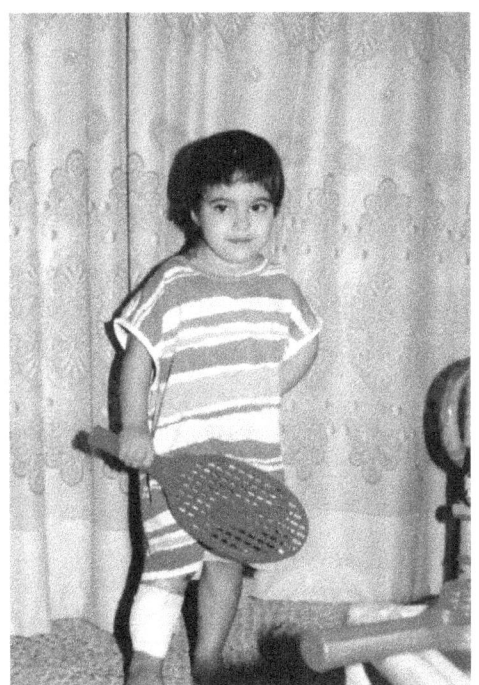

The hand behind her back – constantly trying to scratch the itch away

Two very graphic photos - a skin graph when she was seven

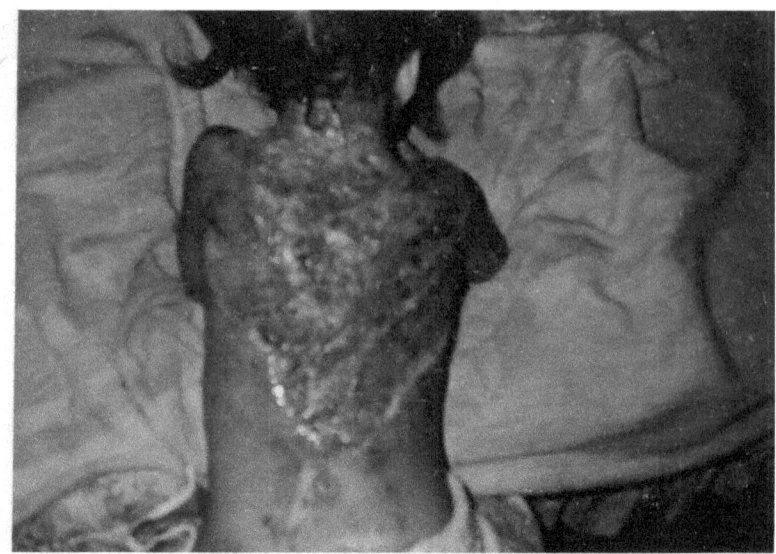

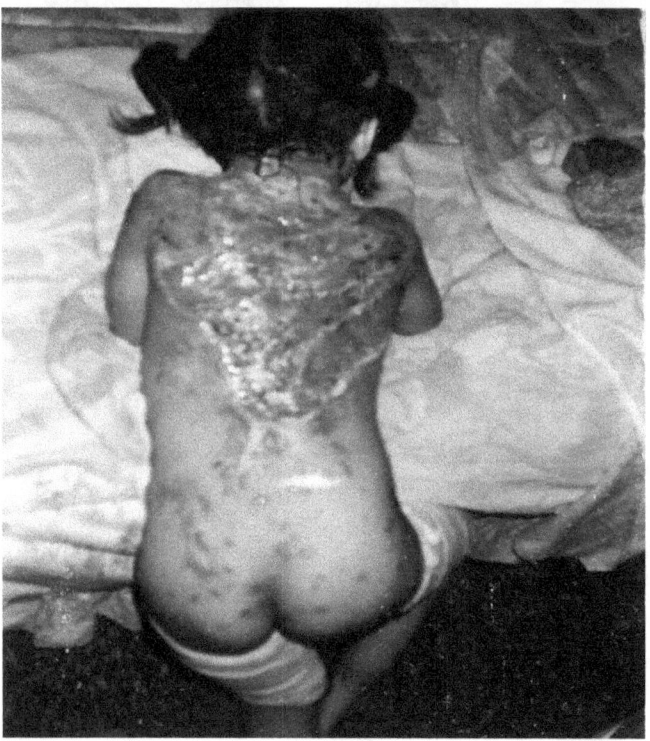

Suffer the little children…

Comparing legs: Two without a mark on them; Two covered in scars

Joy amidst the scars

My annual Christmas wish - to give my healthy skin to someone who needs it more than I do...

www.ingramcontent.com/pod-product-compliance
Lightning Source LLC
Chambersburg PA
CBHW050137170426
43197CB00011B/1868